HOPE LIVES!

A Collection of Devotions and Studies for Individuals and Groups.

To my dear family; your unshakeable love has been my bedrock of strength. I love you with all my heart!

A special word of thanks to Cherry Kater and Elisabeth Atkins for your help in editing this book.

A Collection of Devotions and Studies
for Individuals and Groups
BECAUSE HE LIVES.
Hope
Lives!
Leston Blackburn

HOPE LIVES!

A Collection of Devotions and Studies for Individuals and Groups.

Published by P91 Publications

ISBN: 978-0-9566513-0-3

FOREWORD

How fortunate we are to serve a God whose love is immeasurable, whose grace is extravagant and whose care is immense!

Apart from sending His Son to save us, God has given His Word to instruct us and His Spirit to transform us. Surely such an unwavering and unparalleled commitment from Him deserves, at the very least, a determined and focused response from us.

I pray that you will read each of these reflections prayerfully, and that you, by His grace, would purpose to become the person He sees in you! May we all determine to be lights set on a hill, radiating His glory and revealing His heart to those around us.

Each chapter has been designed to give a brief insight into a portion of Scripture. They can be read and studied either personally or in a group.

Discussion questions follow at the end of the book, which, I trust, will help you as you engage with the Lord and with each other. Be blessed. Be a blessing!

Table of Contents

1

Backs to the Door

Text: Mark 2:1-12

A few days later, when Jesus again entered Capernaum, the people heard that he had come home. So many gathered that there was no room left, not even outside the door, and he preached the word to them. Some men came, bringing to him a paralytic, carried by four of them. Since they could not get him to Jesus because of the crowd, they made an opening in the roof above Jesus and, after digging through it, lowered the mat the paralyzed man was lying on. When Jesus saw their faith, he said to the paralytic, "Son, your sins are forgiven."

Now some teachers of the law were sitting there, thinking to themselves, "Why does this fellow talk like that? He's blaspheming! Who can forgive sins but God alone?"

Immediately Jesus knew in his spirit that this was what they were thinking in their hearts, and he said to them, "Why are you thinking these things? Which is easier: to say to the paralytic, 'Your sins are forgiven,' or to say, 'Get up, take your mat and walk'? But that you may know that the Son of Man has authority on earth to forgive sins . . . ." He said to the paralytic, "I tell you, get up, take your mat and go home." He got up, took his mat and walked out in full view of them all. This amazed everyone and they praised God, saying, "We have never seen anything like this!"

I once read about a remarkable incident that allegedly took place during the First World War. If it is a true account, then I believe it is one of the best examples of indomitable love and selfless courage in action. Let me explain.

The Great War was, in the main, a war fought in the trenches. It was an extremely arduous struggle where men were made to fight for every inch of ground gained. In between the trenches was an area called 'No-Man's Land'. It was given this unenviable title for the simple reason that those who ventured into this inhospitable terrain seldom stayed long enough to occupy it. With bombs dropping all around and bullets whizzing overhead, men were made to overcome all sorts of obstacles in their frenzied dash to capture the enemy's lines.

Among other things, relentless stretches of barbed wire spanned the length of this 'in-between world' like ferocious fangs, making any kind of advance extremely arduous and unforgiving. It was not surprising to hear of men getting caught on the barbs in their attempts to storm a trench. Almost all of these attacks were unsuccessful, and often the inevitable command was given to sound the retreat. Those who were still alive and able to withdraw did so. But many lay trapped between trenches - dead or dying.

On one such occasion a young German soldier had been caught on the barbed-wire fence. Badly wounded and unable to extricate himself, he hung suspended between life and death, scared and screaming. His chilling cries (and the cries of other soldiers like him) haunted friend and foe alike. It must have been unbearable. Sadly, these screams would often continue unabated for hours. It appeared that this day would be no different.

But then something extraordinary happened. A young American soldier, deeply moved by his suffering foe, decided that he could no longer loiter in the safety of his trench and do nothing. Enemy or not, he felt compelled to respond. With unwavering compassion, he resolutely jumped out of his trench and started to leopard-crawl towards the young German soldier. At once the firing started up again. But when the American officer realised what was going on, he ordered his troops to stop shooting. Puzzled by the sudden lull, the German officer reciprocated.

Moving carefully to where his injured adversary lay, the young man cut the German soldier free before carrying him over to the German trench, placing him in the arms of his commanding officer. Then he turned to make his way back to the safety of his lines. Suddenly he was ordered to halt. Turning around, he noticed that the German officer had stood to attention... to salute him!

It is a wonderful story. Whether it is true or not, I do not know. But I do know of a true account in the gospel of Mark that resembles the same selfless, indomitable devotion. It is the story of a group of men who are introduced to us simply as 'friends of the paralytic'. Without any thought for personal gain, they placed their own fears and uncertainties aside and chose to respond to the desperate need of a helpless friend with uncompromising conviction.

Knowing that Jesus was in town (and having heard about His ability to heal the sick and raise the dead), the friends of the paralytic placed him on a stretcher and carried him what may well have been a considerable distance to the house where Jesus was teaching.

However, when they arrived, their attempts to get to Jesus were hampered by the throngs of people blocking the doorway, clambering to get a glimpse of this great Man of God. I love the way *The Message* puts it:

> *"A crowd gathered, jamming the entrance so no one could get in or out." (Mark 2:2)* [1]

Realising that there would be no way through the crowds, yet refusing to simply walk away, they set about doing the only thing they could think to do - breaking through the roof!

Accessing the roof would not prove too taxing; houses in Capernaum were usually flat-roofed with stairways leading up the side. Breaking through the roof, however, would be a different matter entirely. To ensure that a house was watertight, branches would be placed on top of the crossbeams and then sealed with thick layers of clay. So in order to get through the roof, the friends would have to dig through the clay, remove the branches and lower the stretcher between the beams. It would be noisy, it would be messy and to top it all, it would make them extremely unpopular! Not only would the friends have to placate the outraged owner, but they would also have to weather the angry glares and inevitable hostilities of those who were trying to listen to what Jesus had to say!

But the friends had not come this far simply to be foiled by fuss or abrogated by aggravation. Like the young soldier, they were presented with a choice - and they chose to do whatever they could. Breaking through the roof, they lowered their broken friend to the feet of Christ - and stood in awe as Jesus lifted him to his feet!

The True Mark of Love

How did this profound act of love impact the people gathered in the house? One would be forgiven for thinking that it would spark a turning point in their hearts, awakening a deep desire to selflessly serve and love others in the same way. Sadly, it did not. In fact, no sooner had the paralytic been lowered to the ground than a theological debate erupted.

Unmoved by the commitment of the friends and unconcerned about the plight of the paralytic, the scribes became unhinged by the words of Jesus. He saw a man in need of forgiveness. They simply saw red. Instead of recognising the compassion of God, they became offended by the God of Compassion. "How can this fellow blaspheme like this?" they raged. "Who is he to forgive men their sins?"

I have no doubt that the scribes considered themselves to be among the spiritual elite of their generation. Yet of all those gathered there that day, these 'devout' followers of God were, in reality, furthest from Him. The friends showed compassion; they showed contempt. Christ offered pardon; they offered prejudice. With hardened hearts and darkened minds, these 'men of God' ignored the miracle of God and chose instead to condemn the Son of God.

Jesus, knowing immediately what they were thinking, seized the opportunity to speak truth - but He did much more than that - He chose to cleanse a broken soul and heal a battered body! Stretching out His hands of love while speaking out His words of life, Jesus helped the man to his feet.

It is a wonderful example of love in action. True love doesn't look at circumstances and see opportunities for debate – instead, it discerns a need and purposes to make a difference. Whenever love is confronted with the choice to do something or nothing, love acts! Love responds! Love does not stand fists clenched, arguments at the ready. It is compelled to *do*!

Revealing the Way or Blocking it?

Of course, there is a further question to consider because there was another group of people gathered in the house that day (after all, not everyone had assembled to argue with Jesus). Have you ever wondered who was standing in the doorway, and, more to the point, why they never moved? Why was it necessary for the friends to go up to the roof in the first place? Why didn't the people in the doorway simply stand aside and let them through?

Now at first glance a house packed full of people appears to be an exciting proposition. No doubt several of those gathered had done so enthusiastically, eager to hear and see the One of whom so many had spoken. After all, He taught with an authority that few had dreamed possible. His ability to perform the miraculous had become legendary. How wonderful it was to have a doorway jammed full of people eager to hear Christ, eager to see Him at work.

But what if you were one of the friends wanting to bring your broken friend to Christ? Now I would imagine that the friends would have tried to get in to the house through the doorway first, given that they were clearly so determined, so desperate to get their friend to Jesus. I am equally certain that some of the people standing in the doorway would have understood what they were trying to do. Here were four men carrying a man on a stretcher to the very Person who had healed so many. Surely the logical thing to do would be to make room. Yet they didn't. Why not?

Why was it necessary for the friends to climb onto the roof in the first place? Why were they forced to go to such extreme lengths as to dig through a roof at a public gathering? Because they realised they had to!

Is it possible that the people refused to stand aside? After all, Jesus was in town, and they weren't going to miss their moment with Him!

Backs to the World

How wonderful to see a crowd gathered to listen to Jesus. How sad to see a crowd insensitive to the needs around them!

Wanting to hear the voice of the Master is noble indeed. But what if we do so backs to the door, not wanting to give up our seats, not wanting to be personally inconvenienced for the sake of others?

How sad to think that some of us, the very people of God, may well gather enthusiastically Sunday after Sunday to learn about the Shepherd who promised to leave the ninety-nine to look for the one lost sheep, yet do so backs to the door, backs to the world as we listen.

It is sobering to consider that we, the very people identified by the name of Christ, may well be guilty of discerning the need of a broken world yet not caring enough to face up to our responsibility to go, to bring them to Jesus. Now we may listen eagerly, intently, enthusiastically. We may even debate impressively. But do we care sufficiently? Are we, His Church, truly being His hands and His feet? Are we, like Jesus, being a friend to sinners, or do we prefer to be judge and jury?

Are we so eagerly learning about Christ that we have neglected to follow Him? Do we still believe that He makes all the difference in the world, enough so to be prepared to inconvenience ourselves, to sacrifice our comforts, to face up to the inevitable criticisms for the sake of having broken friends made whole by Him? Are we prepared to do whatever it takes to bring them to Jesus? Or would we rather stand in the doorways, huddle in the corners, excuses ready and arguments honed?

Three groups gathered that day, the contentious, the captivated and the compassionate. But how do we, His modern-day Church respond? Would God recognise us as people who know how to argue but who cannot see a person in need of healing? Or would He see us as people who have gathered enthusiastically, honourably, nobly, to hear from Him... only to stand, backs to the door, blind to the world, unmoved by the needs around us, unwilling to stand aside? Are we so eager to hear from God that we refuse to give up our time with Jesus, to go when He says, "Go."?

Are our ears truly open to the cries of our villages? Are our hearts open to the needs of our towns? Or do we stand backs to the world, not necessarily oblivious to their cries so much as indifferent, too calloused to be inconvenienced for fear that we might somehow miss out on *our* moment with our Master?

We need to remember that we have not been called to *do* Church; we have been called to *be* Church, and there is a monumental difference between the two. Time spent with Christ should and must conform and transform us until the love we see in God and the love we have for God puts feet to our faith.

The Friends Reached Down so that Jesus Could Reach Out

Is it possible that we have become a Church that spends far more time debating how to decorate the roof rather than how to break through it? In our desire to become more relevant, are we guilty of changing the style yet ignoring the substance? Our facilities, our programs, our agendas are wonderful - providing they cultivate in us an insatiable desire both to know God more *and* to make Him known. If however, they cause us to stand backs to the world, jealously guarding our domain, then are we not just as guilty as those who blocked the doorway to Christ?

How privileged we are to gather freely in the name of Jesus Christ. How honoured we are to be able to worship Him, to fellowship around His Word.

How vital it is to do so. But we must not forget that Christianity is about *following* Christ, about listening rather than simply learning; about obeying rather than simply agreeing. And He has left us with an incredible responsibility – to *go* into all the world and make disciples of all nations... from Jerusalem, to Judea, to Samaria and to the very ends of the earth.

The friends of the paralytic *went* because they knew that their friend was powerless to come to Christ on his own. Their love compelled them to go. They reached down so that Jesus could reach out so that the friend could reach up!

If in our desire to learn more about Jesus, we stand with our backs to the door, if Church becomes about how *we* can benefit, what *we* can gain, if we lose sight of the missionary heart of God, then we are no different to the people who considered their need to hear Jesus as being paramount to the paralytic's need to be touched by Jesus. If we do not own the same compassion and care as the friends of the paralytic, then we may be standing in the right place but with the wrong heart. If that is the case, then no matter how noble our intentions may be, we have missed the whole point!

Jesus is Never Irrelevant

Why is it that church in our generation, *our* generation, is perceived by so many as being irrelevant and unimportant? Why is it that people like Josh McDowell are being led to write books titled, 'The *Last* Christian Generation?'

Is it because the Gospel has lost its power? No! Is it because Jesus is less relevant in our day? No, of course not! Jesus is always relevant! While there is still one person in need of saving grace, there still a need for the One True Saviour!

The early Church exploded into being during a time marked by indisputable secularism, inescapable idolatry and irrefutable sin. Yet the very gates of hell could not stop its advance.

But then the early Church was both upward looking *and* outward looking. They hungered *after* God in order to make a difference *for* God! They understood that being empowered by God was not about the moment, but about the mission. They waited until they had received power from on high, not for the sake of the experience, but because of an insatiable desire to obey Him, a hunger to go and be effective witnesses for Him, bringing the broken to Him regardless of the personal cost.

Jesus Forgave the Paralytic Before He Healed Him

We can be sure that Jesus never came to entertain us. He never healed the man because He wanted to impress the crowd. Jesus is no celebrity and church is no concert. Jesus healed the paralytic because He loved him.

But before Christ touched his *body*, He touched his *soul*. Jesus forgave the paralytic *before* He healed him. Why? Because when all is said and done, our Saviour's priority is our salvation. God knew that the world needed saving, so He came as Saviour!

Regardless of what ministry Christ may have called us to, our hearts should yearn for people to know Him. Paul told Timothy the pastor to fulfil his ministry by doing the work of an evangelist. God never intended His Church to be an institution with doors shut to the world outside. If ever we get to a place where we would rather stand in the doorway than determine to bring broken friends to The Way, then it is time to examine our hearts!

Let me share a story with you. A young lady went to a gospel concert featuring a famous Christian band. During the concert, she was totally and radically saved and sold out for God. The next year she took several of her friends with her because she was desperate for them to come to know God as she had done. Unfortunately she could not get in. Try as she might, her efforts were met with the same response: "Sorry, we're full!"

People who had already bought tickets were queuing to get in. Many were Christians. She was sure that if she asked some of them to give up their seats so that her friends could have an opportunity to come to know Jesus, they would. And so she went up and down the queue, explaining her plight, ever-hopeful that someone would listen. But nobody was going to miss this incredible opportunity to hear such a talented band performing live!

Not to be deterred, she eventually found herself in the car park stopping cars as they entered, literally begging, pleading with people to give up their seat for the sake of her friends. She carried on for three hours until she had enough tickets! It sounds a bit like the friends of the paralytic to me!

I believe that if a few more Christians today cared enough to leave the comfort of our trenches, passionate enough to run up and down car parks, compassionate enough to carry the broken and the lost to Christ, to do whatever it takes to give people the opportunity to discover our awesome Saviour, then I have no doubt that God would do something incredible in our day. We would see broken lives made whole and communities transformed, because our God *is* an awesome God!

And He has chosen us to be His means of provision to our generation. If we will only go, if we will only speak in His name, He *will* transform lives!

A Nation in Need

And our nation needs transforming. Paul Alexander, Dean of Mattersey Bible College shared that the United Kingdom has:

- The fourth biggest economy in the world
- A population of around 60 million people
- Yet the average size of an evangelical church is just 55 people.
- If the current trend of decline continues, by 2020 the average size of an evangelical congregation will be between 16 and 17 people.
- The average age will be 68.
- At present, there are reportedly less people per capita attending church in the UK than there are in countries like Egypt. [2]

The statistics make for depressing reading. What is true of Britain may well be true of many other western countries which were once mission-sending powerhouses.

But there is something far more concrete than statistics: Jesus has promised that the fields are ripe for the harvest and has invited us to lift our eyes and see; He has assured us that He will build His Church and that the very gates of hell will be powerless to stop the advance.

We cannot choose the times we live in any more than could the friends of the paralytic, but we can choose *how* we respond. Now we may feel insignificant, inadequate, incapable of making any meaningful difference. But we are not the ones who make the difference - our role is simply to bring people to Christ so that *He* can be the difference! We *can* do that! We *must* do that!

The consequence of doing nothing is always worse in the long term than the consequence of doing something for God, even if what we do seems insignificant in our eyes. It doesn't help waiting until we feel we are ready to make a difference for Jesus. I can tell you that we never *feel* ready. It is about grasping each moment that presents itself and purposing to be His hands and His feet. It is about doing all that we can when the situation arises, trusting God to do the rest. Oswald Chambers once said:

> "We must never put our dreams of success as God's purpose for us; His purpose may be exactly the opposite. We have the idea that God is leading us to a particular end, a desired goal; He is not. The question of getting to a particular end is a mere incident. What we call process, God calls the end.
>
> "... It is the process, not the end, which is glorifying to God. God's training is for now, not presently. His purpose is for this minute, not for something in the future. We have nothing to do with the afterwards of obedience; we get it wrong when we think of the afterwards." [3]

The friends saw a need. They knew that Jesus was the answer and they knew that they had to do something to make a difference. So they put the paralytic on a stretcher and brought him to the One who makes all the difference!

They might not have been as well versed in the Scriptures as the religious leaders gathered there that day; they might not have enjoyed the same vantage point as the people standing in the doorway. But what they did have was the simple ability to share the load, to carry a friend... and the joy of seeing Jesus become his everything!

Four friends brought wholeness to a broken man and glory to God. That is what Christianity is about. That is something we are all qualified to do! Will you step out of the doorway? Will you allow God to do something awesome in response to your simple acts of selfless love? Oh, I hope so!

2

Who do You Say I Am?

Text: Mark 8:27-33

Jesus and his disciples went on to the villages around Caesarea Philippi. On the way he asked them, "Who do people say I am?" They replied, "Some say John the Baptist; others say Elijah; and still others, one of the prophets."

"But what about you?" he asked. "Who do you say I am?" Peter answered, "You are the Christ."

Jesus warned them not to tell anyone about him.

He then began to teach them that the Son of Man must suffer many things and be rejected by the elders, chief priests and teachers of the law, and that he must be killed and after three days rise again. He spoke plainly about this, and Peter took him aside and began to rebuke him.

But when Jesus turned and looked at his disciples, he rebuked Peter. "Get behind me, Satan!" he said. "You do not have in mind the things of God, but the things of men."

Jesus impacted people wherever He went. Whether they approved of Him or resented Him, Jesus made an indelible impression. Some adored Him. Some despised Him. Few, if any, remained indifferent.

There were those who were overwhelmed with amazement, astounded both by the miracles He did and by the authority with which He taught. Others believed Him to be a great man. The rich young ruler (a man of influence himself) addressed Jesus as 'Good Teacher.' Still others believed Christ to be a prophet, possibly Elijah, possibly John the Baptist come back from the dead. Some held sinister views, claiming Him to be a demoniac who operated by the power of Beelzebub. Whether people loved Him or loathed Him, all were challenged to define Him! This is not surprising, of course, because it is difficult to remain indifferent where Christ is concerned.

What is more, Jesus stated clearly that our understanding of Him is the very point which will decide our eternity; it is as central to our destiny as it is to Mark's gospel, and, as such, it is a question which demands a personal response. Of course, it will never suffice to simply know what others think - each one of us must consider the evidence about Him and decide for ourselves who we believe Him to be.

It therefore comes as no surprise to read an account of Christ challenging His disciples to ponder what others were saying about Him before affirming who *they* believed Him to be. "Who do people say I am? Who do *you* say I am?"

The Man Who Saw, Yet Did Not See

Peter does not disappoint - he was quick off the mark as usual! Revealing his conviction that Jesus was the very Anointed One promised by God, Peter answered, "You are the Christ." He was right of course, and if the conversation had ended there, all would have been well. But Peter's understanding of what his proclamation of faith implied was sketchy at best. By his very next statement, Peter revealed that he had a partial understanding of Christ's Messianic role at best. As Jesus began to teach about His impending death and resurrection, the very heartbeat of His ministry, Peter took Him aside... to *rebuke* Him!

While Peter believed Christ to be the Messiah, talk of death was too inconceivable to even contemplate. That Christ was the Messiah was beyond doubt as far as Peter was concerned, but to have a Messiah who spoke of dying simply would not do. After all, this concept conflicted with his preconception of a Messiah who would come to Israel's rescue riding victoriously on a white horse. No! As far as Peter was concerned, Jesus, the Messiah, needed correcting. And it was best that he, Christ's most 'loyal subject' should be the one to say so.

Never afraid to express an opinion, Peter took Jesus aside (as though this somehow made the public correction more palatable) and rebuked Him! Peter the sinner rebuked Christ the Saviour! Peter saw. He saw more clearly than many had. Yet clearly, Peter did not see!

Of course, it wouldn't be fair to pick on Peter. The truth is that none of the disciples had truly grasped who Jesus really was. If they had truly understood who was standing in their midst, none would have deserted Him, none would have denied Him, none would have ended up hiding behind locked doors for fear of their lives.

Like Peter, the disciples had reached a conclusion about Jesus. He was indeed the Christ, the Anointed One of God. But, like Peter, they only understood in part; they saw, yet, in reality, they did not see.

Transformed Lives

They would come to understand fully, of course - but not this day. It would only be after several encounters with the risen Christ that a group of confused, broken, bewildered, fearful disciples would be transformed into mighty men of faith who would be used by God to turn the world upside down. In time there would be no doubting who they believed Him to be!

Yes, the disciples would see; they would understand - but not this day. It would only be after the resurrected Jesus had opened their minds that they would fully grasp who stood before them. Luke reveals that their eyes would be opened only *after* the risen Saviour stood in their midst:

> *Then He opened their minds so they could understand the Scriptures. (Luke 24:45)*

Saul Encounters the Christ

What about Saul? A man who started a journey to Damascus convinced that he was fulfilling God's destiny for his life came face to face with the risen Christ only to discover how mistaken he had been! Zealously defending what he perceived to be obedience to the Law (and therefore obedience to God as he understood it), Saul had unwittingly ended up persecuting the very Author of faith! Like Peter, Saul was convinced that his perception of Christ was correct. Like Peter, Saul was sincere in his convictions. Like Peter, Saul was sincerely wrong!

But Saul *too* would see. Jesus would appear to Saul just as He had appeared to the Eleven. He would open Saul's eyes just as He had opened theirs. Saul came to understand that he was a man who claimed to see, yet was blind. Ironically, after seeing the vision of Christ, he would be a man who was blind, yet able to see!

> *"Who are You, Lord?" Saul asked. "I am Jesus, whom you are persecuting," He replied. (Acts 9:5)*

Conviction and Zeal Are Not Enough

Two great men of God, Peter and Paul (Saul), saw and understood the Christ for the first time only when *He* opened their eyes! If conviction were enough, both would have been lauded for their faith. Both men were convinced about who they believed Him to be. Both came to Christ with preconceived convictions, opinions and interpretations. Both were mistaken.

If conviction were enough, neither would have been found wanting. If zeal were the measure, neither would have been rebuked. But zeal alone is never enough. They had to answer the central question - and answer it correctly; "Who do you say I Am?"

The sobering reality is that both had claimed to have walked with God. The lesson is clear; if Peter and Paul could get it so monumentally wrong, could the same not be true of us? Is it possible that we hold preconceptions of Christ that are less than accurate?

Shaken, not Stirred

Who do we say that He is? How closely does our *opinion* of Him match the reality of *who* He truly is? If we are to see Jesus *as* He is, and not as we *think* He is, then we need to be prepared to have Him shake our opinions, challenge our convictions and reshape our prejudices. What good is it to be zealous, yet mistaken?

It is never enough to hold a view of Christ that is less than who He is! The rich young ruler saw Him as a good man. It was not enough. Jesus is far more than a good man.

Others believed Him to be a prophet. It was not enough. Some, like Peter, believed Him to be the Messiah, but held a view of Him that was fashioned by *their* perceptions, clouded by *their* convictions and biased by *their* prejudices. It was not enough.

It was inadequate then and it is inadequate now; we must see Jesus as He *is*, not as we *think* He is! And this is only possible through an encounter with Him. Who do you say that He is?

Who Shapes Your View?

How is it possible that so many people, sincere as they were, could be so mistaken about Christ? How could people from the same generation, the same nation, the same era, studying the same Scriptures, end up with such sharply divided views of Christ and such different interpretations of the texts? How could some shout, "Demoniac" while others exclaimed, "Messiah" - and even then, hold an understanding of the Messiah that excluded the cross and fell so inadequately short of the mark?

The only logical conclusion is that people approached Jesus based on *their* perceptions, *their* prejudices, *their* reasoning and *their* logic, as if the final authority somehow rested with *them* and not with *Him.* And if it is God who opens our minds to the Scriptures (as I believe it is), then their approach was flawed from the very outset.

The reality is that we cannot approach Christ claiming to know Him fully. Like Peter, like Paul, like everyone else for that matter, we all approach Christ having opinions and perceptions clouded by our experiences, cluttered by our culture and our contexts. We may have an opinion of Him (and it is important to have one), but we must bear in mind that it is merely *our* opinion.

The reality is that we are people in search of truth. We are not, however, the authors *of* truth. Even the most devout of followers, like Peter, get it horribly wrong when they try to understand Him as *they* are and not as *He* is! It is essential that we ask God to open our minds to understand truth as He sees it rather than try and fashion God to fit neatly into our perceptions of truth. After all, God *is* Truth!

Peter could never have done great things for God while he believed he understood Jesus better than Jesus did! Paul could never have had the impact on the world that he did if he had remained steadfast in his preconceptions of Christ. Peter needed Jesus to open his eyes.

If our ability to see is in the hands of God, then we need to be prepared to allow God to enable us to see. This may mean laying down a few worldviews, but I would rather see clearly and be considered blind by my generation than be blind and yet *presume* that I can see! And the reality is that we all come to Christ with preconceptions and worldviews, whether we like it or not. However, let us be sure not to leave that way!

Modern-Day Interpretations: More of the Same

When all is said and done, modern opinions don't differ as vastly from Bible times as we may think. There are still people today who do not see Jesus as the Christ. Some still speak ill of Him. There are those who still believe Him to be a prophet or a good man at best.

But it is also my firm conviction that there are still many who, like Peter, see Jesus as the Christ, yet who cannot accept His teaching without a need to correct Him on a few issues. After all, *surely* what He says cannot be truth if it doesn't line up with what *we* believe...

In a modern world built and bent on political correctness, naturalism and relativism, are we guilty of coming to God with pre-conceived ideas in the hope of getting Him to change *His* mind rather than accepting the need to change *ours*? Is it possible that we, like Peter, look at the Scriptures and feel the need to draw God aside to *'put Him in the picture'* on a few things?

And in case you think this isn't pertinent to you, ask yourself: When the Scriptures differ from your modern interpretations, do you surrender your views or do you try to re-define the Scriptures?

Peter wanted a Messiah fashioned after his own understanding. Jesus, however, would not accommodate him. He could not; He is Truth! As difficult as it may be to comprehend, the fact is that Peter deserved the rebuke he received:

> *Jesus turned and said to Peter, "Get behind me, Satan! You are a stumbling block to me; you do not have in mind the things of God, but the things of men." (Matthew 16:23)*

Do we have in mind the things of God or do we still embrace the opinions of men? Are we, as Christians, guilty of trying to move the plumb-line of God's Word in an attempt to be relevant? Are we guilty of trying to interpret the Word in a way that is more palatable to our generation? If so, then all we will succeed in doing is becoming relative rather than relevant!

The danger, of course, is that truth as we see it becomes relative when we move the boundary markers. Who ends up deciding what is right and what is wrong? Who decides what is acceptable and what isn't?

It has been suggested that there are something like 20,000 different Christian organisations, groups, denominations, para-church ministries and networks in existence today. On some level, each group interprets parts of the Scriptures differently. Just like the people in the times of Christ's earthly ministry, we have a broad range of opinions about a broad range of issues. Yet we live in the same times, claim to follow the same God, and read the same Bible. Why is that?

And what is more alarming is the fact that doctrines and opinions don't only differ from denomination to denomination, or organisation to organisation, but within denominations and organisations. Sometimes we become so dogmatic about our beliefs that we choose to have nothing to do with any group that believes differently. But if Jesus is *the* Way, *the* Truth and *the* Life, and we as Christians claim to be following Him, how is it possible that we can have such vastly different opinions and interpretations in the Church today? Is it possible that we have fallen prey to the same aberration as Peter, as Paul? Is it possible that we are governed by our views rather than Christ's teachings?

Does He Change Our Minds or do We Try to Change His?

How is it that we so conveniently adopt opinions and interpretations that more closely resemble our own? If Jesus is the One with the power and authority to open minds (and I believe He is), then are we allowing Him to open our minds to see as He sees, or are we so convinced that our views are correct that we set about trying to open His mind instead? If so, are we any different to Peter? Are we any less deserving of the same scathing rebuke from Christ?

Is it possible that we, like Saul, hold views that actually set us at odds against the very God we claim to serve and follow? Do we accept what God says in His Word, or do we feel the need to draw our Messiah aside from time to time and tell Him to adopt a view that is more in keeping with what we consider to be accurate, or palatable? If so, we have made a grave error of judgement. If that be the case, then it is my firm conviction that *we* need to re-visit His pivotal question: "Who do you say that I Am?"

How We See Christ Impacts *How* We See

The truth is that the disciples did not see Jesus for who He is because they were *unable* to see. They read the Scriptures yet failed to grasp what they were reading because they did not have the ability *to* grasp! It was only after the resurrected Jesus opened their minds that they were able *to* see:

> *Then He opened their minds so they could understand the Scriptures. (Luke 24:45)*

Before this life-changing encounter with Christ, His life-changing teachings had some impact, but failed to have complete impact. It is how we see Jesus that determines our ability *to* see!

So how do we see Jesus? Do we see Him as our resurrected Lord? Have we entered into His presence and allowed Him to open our minds so that we can understand the Scriptures?

Truth is not a journey of discovery that leads to Christ. Truth *is* the Person of Christ! He *is* Truth, and as such He alone has the power to open our minds. If we are to understand, then *He* must be our Alpha! If we truly believe that Jesus is our Messiah, our Master, our Lord, our Foundation, then shouldn't we give Him the opportunity to open our minds, to conform them as He sees fit, not to try and change His mind and His Word to match our views?

Is He your foundation, your starting point? Is He your Alpha? Do you begin at His feet and say, "Open my mind Lord!" or, like Peter, do you say, "Messiah, I need to correct You on a few issues!" When all is said and done, faith is much like life. It doesn't start with us. True faith is a response to what God has initiated. Faith is not true faith if God has not authored it. He is, after all, the author, initiator and perfecter of our faith.

Faith in a Modern World

In a world that prides itself on reason, logic, knowledge and naturalism, faith is not exactly the best of bedfellows. Faith makes no sense in our times. Reason looks at the natural and draws logical, reasonable conclusions. But faith is *un*reasonable. It does not view God as natural but as *super*-natural. It does not attempt to measure His thoughts by our thoughts. Faith does not try to define God and the things of God by our neat, comfortable, convenient definitions, willing only to acquiesce at best. God doesn't give us that option. If He truly is our foundation, if He truly is the author and perfecter of our faith, the One with the power to open minds, then we have to begin the process at His feet rather than expect Him to begin at ours!

To the mind fashioned in modern times, a God who speaks the universe into being is inconceivable; a God who leads a man to build an ark is implausible. To such a mind, a God who becomes a Man to take the sins of humankind upon Himself is illogical. It may well be that we are, in part, the product of our times, coloured by the perceptions and prejudices of the day, that we have unwittingly fashioned world views that are inconsistent with Scripture at best.

But what do we do when the shoe simply will not fit comfortably? Do we allow God to change *our* minds, or do we try and change the Scriptures to *make* them fit? If so, are we not doing precisely what Peter did – fashioning a Messiah after *our* understanding? No, faith must, by virtue of being faith, begin at the feet of Christ!

Who Do You Say that He Is?

We cannot treat God like some souped-up sports car – wonderful to have around provided we get to decide the specs! God is not a commodity to be fashioned; He is God to be worshipped, and followed! He doesn't bend to our definition of Him. We don't get to choose 'some' of Him. The question He posed to His disciples is the question He puts to us: "Who do you say that I Am?"

We may be comfortable with Jesus the Saviour because we know we need saving. But when we get Jesus, we get the *whole* of Jesus! The same Saviour who gives His life for us also tells us to love our enemies, to take up our cross and follow Him, to forgive others if we want to be forgiven. This may not sit very comfortably with us. But that should not surprise us. After all, God's main objective is not our comfort.

Neither do we get to choose which 'version' of Jesus we want to follow. Not really. Each of us must face up to the same challenge the disciples needed to face up to – who do we say that He is? And once we've expressed an opinion, we need to be open to His correction – we need to get our opinions in line with His Word rather than trying to get His Word to line up with our opinions.

> *For no one can lay a foundation other than that which is laid, which is Jesus Christ.* *(1 Corinthians 3:11)*

> *And let us run with perseverance the race marked out for us, fixing our eyes on Jesus, the pioneer and perfecter of faith.*
>
> *(Hebrews 12:1b-2)*

The Christian's Worldview Should be Christ

What is a worldview? In short, it is a comprehensive perception of the world from a specific standpoint. An individual's worldview is his 'big picture', a harmony, if you will, of all his beliefs about the world. It is his way of understanding reality.

One's worldview is the basis for making daily decisions and is therefore extremely important. *What* we see is determined by *how* we see. Somebody once described it as follows: An apple sitting on a table is seen by several people. A botanist, looking at the apple, may want to classify it. An artist will want to paint it. A child may want to eat it.

How we see and interpret the world around us is influenced and shaped by how we see the world at large. A naturalistic worldview generates many related philosophies such as moral relativism, utopianism, pragmatism or existentialism. But for the Christian, *Christ* must be our worldview!

> The Bible never distinguishes between a "religious" and a "secular" life; the Christian life is the only life there is. Jesus proclaimed Himself "the way, the truth, and the life" and, in doing so, became our worldview.[4]

We can't approach God saying, "I believe *this*, now let me interpret *You*." We need to approach Him saying, "I believe *You*, now help me understand *this*." To build on a lesser foundation than God Himself will always be to build on sand.

We must allow God, through the working of His Spirit and the Scriptures, to shape our thinking. As valuable as human knowledge is, it is not the pinnacle of all things. Love, for one thing, surpasses knowledge. And *God* is love!

> *... to know this love that surpasses knowledge – that you may be filled to the measure of all the fullness of God. (Ephesians 3:19)*

Put on the Mind of Christ

The solution is to put on the mind of Christ. Making Jesus Christ our foundation is not only Scriptural, it is crucial! It impacts eternity, it impacts life and it impacts our very ability to be able *to* understand. That is why God commands us to put on the mind of Christ.

We do this by going to His Word and allowing it to be to us a lamp to our feet and a light to our path – a lamp to light today and illuminate tomorrow. When confronted with various situations and circumstances, ask yourself not only what God would *do*, but what God has *said*. Consider what God has commanded, and then choose to live accordingly. Why? Times change, and so do the opinions of men. But God remains the same yesterday, today and forever. Paul saw it. Peter saw it. Please Lord, may we see it too!

Scriptures for Further Reflection

> *Do not conform any longer to the pattern of this world, but be transformed by the renewing of your mind. Then you will be able to test and approve what God's will is—his good, pleasing and perfect will. (Romans 12:1-2)*

> *If you have any encouragement from being united with Christ, if any comfort from his love, if any fellowship with the Spirit, if any tenderness and compassion, then make my joy complete by being like-minded, having the same love, being one in spirit and purpose.*
>
> *(Philippians 2:1-2)*

Rather, we have renounced secret and shameful ways; we do not use deception, nor do we distort the word of God. On the contrary, by setting forth the truth plainly we commend ourselves to every man's conscience in the sight of God. And even if our gospel is veiled, it is veiled to those who are perishing. The god of this age has blinded the minds of unbelievers, so that they cannot see the light of the gospel of the glory of Christ, who is the image of God. For we do not preach ourselves, but Jesus Christ as Lord, and ourselves as your servants for Jesus' sake. For God, who said, "Let light shine out of darkness," made his light shine in our hearts to give us the light of the knowledge of the glory of God in the face of Christ.

(2 Corinthians 4:2-6)

So I tell you this, and insist on it in the Lord, that you must no longer live as the Gentiles do, in the futility of their thinking. They are darkened in their understanding and separated from the life of God because of the ignorance that is in them due to the hardening of their hearts. Having lost all sensitivity, they have given themselves over to sensuality so as to indulge in every kind of impurity, with a continual lust for more... You, however, did not come to know Christ that way. Surely you heard of him and were taught in him in accordance with the truth that is in Jesus. You were taught, with regard to your former way of life, to put off your old self, which is being corrupted by its deceitful desires; to be made new in the attitude of your minds; and to put on the new self, created to be like God in true righteousness and holiness.

(Eph 4:17-23)

Since, then, you have been raised with Christ, set your hearts on things above, where Christ is seated at the right hand of God. Set your minds on things above, not on earthly things. For you died, and your life is now hidden with Christ in God. When Christ, who is your life, appears, then you also will appear with him in glory.

(Col 3:1-2)

3

The Man Who Refused to Wear a Label

Text: John 20: 19-29

On the evening of that first day of the week, when the disciples were together, with the doors locked for fear of the Jews, Jesus came and stood among them and said, "Peace be with you!" After he said this, he showed them his hands and side. The disciples were overjoyed when they saw the Lord.

Again Jesus said, "Peace be with you! As the Father has sent me, I am sending you." And with that he breathed on them and said, "Receive the Holy Spirit. If you forgive anyone his sins, they are forgiven; if you do not forgive them, they are not forgiven."

Now Thomas (called Didymus), one of the Twelve, was not with the disciples when Jesus came. So the other disciples told him, "We have seen the Lord!"

But he said to them, "Unless I see the nail marks in his hands and put my finger where the nails were, and put my hand into his side, I will not believe it."

A week later his disciples were in the house again, and Thomas was with them. Though the doors were locked, Jesus came and stood among them and said, "Peace be with you!" Then he said to Thomas, "Put your finger here; see my hands. Reach out your hand and put it into my side. Stop doubting and believe."

Thomas said to him, "My Lord and my God!"

Then Jesus told him, "Because you have seen me, you have believed; blessed are those who have not seen and yet have believed."

Of the many sermons preached about Thomas, most have referred to him in one way or another by the title which has become synonymous with his name: 'Thomas the Doubter', or 'Doubting Thomas.' We have inadvertently given Thomas a label.

But there is far more to Thomas than can be learnt from the opening text, and I believe we do the man a grave injustice when we choose to summarise the whole of his life by one week of weakness. In fact, I believe wholeheartedly that if God were to give Thomas a title to summarise his life, it wouldn't be 'Doubting Thomas.' Let me explain.

The Man (Scriptural Evidence)

Apart from our opening passage, two further portions of Scripture provide a small, yet significant insight into the character of Thomas. John 11 records the death of Lazarus, and more to the point, the reaction of the disciples to the response of Jesus.

When Jesus informed His disciples that He wanted to go back to Judea, the disciples were less than enthusiastic. This is not surprising, of course, because people had wanted to stone Him during His previous visit. Neither aware of the seriousness nor the significance of the occasion, the disciples tried to dissuade Him. But Jesus insisted.

After two more days, Jesus informed His disciples that Lazarus was dead, and that His intention was to go and wake him up. None of the disciples were particularly enthusiastic, it should be said! Yet it is Thomas who speaks up;

> *Then Thomas (called Didymus) said to the rest of the disciples, "Let us also go, that we may die with Him." (John 11:16)*

Now one could argue that Thomas (once again true to character) was simply displaying a lack of faith. But was he? After all, one could just as easily conclude that his comment, while arguably cynical, displayed a willingness to follow Christ even at the very risk of death!

Thomas could not have known the wonderful outcome that awaited them. All he knew was what he had witnessed - the image of people picking up stones to stone Jesus was still fresh in the minds of the disciples. Yet despite this, Thomas is the one who spoke up to encourage the rest to follow Christ, regardless of the risk. And it worked, because follow they did!

John 14 provides another wonderful insight into the character of Thomas. Referring to His imminent death, resurrection and ascension, Jesus taught His disciples that He would go away to prepare a place for them. He would then return to fetch them. As was so often the case, the disciples were yet again incapable of understanding the profundity of what Jesus was saying.

Jesus concludes by saying;

> *"You know the way to the place where I am going."(John 14:4)*

Thomas responded:

> *"We don't know where You are going, so how can we know the way?" (John 14:5)*

Again, it could be argued that Thomas (true to his nature) was expressing more doubt. But is it possible that he was the one man on this occasion with the courage to ask for an explanation? I am sure all the disciples were at a loss as to what Jesus meant. After all, how could they understand the eternal significance of His words when they still battled to grasp the message of the cross - even though Jesus had told them several times that He would die and rise again. Thomas asked what others probably wanted to ask, but didn't! I don't believe these Scriptures support the label. To the contrary, I think they give a very different perspective of the man we have come to know as 'Doubting Thomas.'

The Man (Extra- Biblical Evidence)

History gives us a very different understanding of the man Thomas, revealing just how deeply Christ impacted his life.

You see, what many people don't know is that Thomas faithfully preached the Gospel for forty more years. The last fourteen years of his life was spent on the mission field, far away from the comforts and the familiarities of home. Tradition holds that Thomas planted the very first church in India where he served out the last fourteen years of his life from AD 58 to AD 72 before being martyred for his faith on the hills of Madras!

If God were to give Thomas a title, I doubt very much that it would be 'Doubting Thomas.' Why? Because that would entail labelling his whole life according to the events of one week, and, in the process, to ignore the forty years of faithful service and devotion to Christ that would follow.

No, if God were to give Thomas a label, it wouldn't be 'Doubting Thomas.' It could be 'Thomas the Apostle', or 'Thomas the Church Planter'. It could even be 'Thomas the Missionary' or 'Thomas the Martyr', because all of these labels would be equally true of him.

There is far more to Thomas than a moment or moments of weakness. Indeed, I believe that if God were to give Thomas a title befitting his life, it would be something like, "Thomas: The Man who Finished Well!" I believe it is fair to say that Thomas was a man who refused to live under a label!

Living with Labels

How sad that so many of us live the bulk of our lives under labels we have inherited from days gone by; summarised by a moment, or moments, of weakness, choosing to live out the rest of our days locked behind the closed doors of our past.

This of course is something that affects people from every walk of life. Kings have been remembered by disparaging labels. King Charles of France was known as 'Charles the Simple', son of 'Louis the Stutterer'. Louis the Sluggard, who ruled over the Franks from 986 AD to 987 AD, was noted for his self-indulgence. Then there was 'Ethelred the Unready', the leader who was unable to repel the Danish invasion of England. And let us not forget 'Louis the Fat', a title given to a king who allegedly was no longer able to mount his horse by the age of 47 because of his rather large frame.

And here is a man of God whom we conveniently remember as 'Doubting Thomas.' We live in a world that constantly labels us! We label each other so easily. Sadly, we wear those labels so readily.

Luanne Oleas shares a rather amusing story about labels:

> When the 1960's ended, San Francisco's Haight-Ashbury district reverted to high rent, and many hippies moved down the coast to Santa Cruz. They had children and got married, too, though in no particular sequence. But they didn't name their children Melissa or Brett. People in the mountains around Santa Cruz grew accustomed to their children playing Frisbee with little *Time Warp* or *Spring Fever*. And eventually *Moonbeam, Earth, Love* and *Precious Promise* all ended up in public school.
>
> That's when the kindergarten teachers first met Fruit Stand. Every fall, according to tradition, parents bravely apply name tags to their children, kiss them good-bye and send them off to school on the bus. So it was for Fruit Stand. The teachers thought the boy's name was odd, but they tried to make the best of it.
>
> "Would you like to play with the blocks, *Fruit Stand*?" they offered. And later, "*Fruit Stand*, how about a snack?" He accepted hesitantly. By the end of the day, his name didn't seem much stranger than Heather's or Sun Ray's.
>
> At dismissal time, the teachers led the children out to the buses. "*Fruit Stand*, do you know which one is your bus?"
>
> He didn't answer. That wasn't strange. He hadn't answered them all day. Lots of children are shy on the first day of school. It didn't matter. Now the teachers had also instructed the parents to write the names of their children's bus stops on the reverse side of their name tags. The teacher simply turned over *Fruit Stand's* tag. There, neatly printed, was the name *Anthony*. [5]

Labels are dangerous indeed! Thomas has been labelled by us – but not by God! He doesn't remember Thomas that way!

Jesus came personally to restore him. He came to show Thomas that he had a future in Jesus that was far greater than his past! He came to show Thomas that his destiny was not his history!

The Moment

Now that we have considered the man Thomas, let us turn our attention to the moment he doubted. What is it that brought Thomas to the brink of despair? What had Thomas experienced that caused him to declare that he could not believe unless He saw Christ with his own eyes and touched Him with his own hands?

Well, let us think about it for a moment. Thomas had left everything to follow Jesus - his bridges had been burnt so to speak. Now, the very Person in whom he had invested his life, was gone - dead and buried (or so he thought)!

I wonder how *we* would have responded had we been confronted with the same situation.

The reality is that all the disciples were gripped by doubt and fear, not only Thomas. Every disciple doubted. If they had truly believed, none would have been sitting in fear and shame behind locked doors in the first place!

But it seems that Thomas was that much more desperate, disillusioned and discouraged than the others. They took comfort in the company of each other. Thomas had separated himself for a time. When Jesus visited them the first time, Thomas was absent.

He was a man in despair. Being caught in this confusing 'in-between time' that Jesus had warned about proved too much for him. And so, with heart broken and head bowed, Thomas lost hope.

Then, when Thomas was reunited with the disciples, he heard exciting reports that the Christ had appeared to them, just as He promised. But he had heard this all before. After all, the ladies had come to the disciples previously, excited at having seen the risen Christ. The disciples hadn't believed the women then, so why should Thomas now believe them now?

Their excitement in telling Thomas, like Mary's joy in telling them, did nothing to convince him. He wanted to see for himself as they had done. He wanted to experience for himself, as did they, if he was to trust again, believe again. He was caught in a crisis of faith. Nothing and no-one but Jesus Himself would be able to restore his shattered hope.

But Jesus had already been. Jesus was there; Thomas was not. God Almighty had showed up, but Thomas had been absent.

Of course, he was not the first person in Scripture to doubt, to question God. There have been many living in that in-between moment. Read the Psalms and you will see several examples of men grappling with their faith in times of distress. Read the account written by Habakkuk and you will hear more than a man questioning – you will actually hear a man complaining to God until he came to understand, and subsequently pen, one of the most profound declarations of unwavering faith:

> *Though the fig tree does not bud and there are no grapes on the vines, though the olive crop fails and the fields produce no food, though there are no sheep in the pen and no cattle in the stalls, yet I will rejoice in the Lord, I will be joyful in God my Saviour. The Sovereign Lord is my strength; He makes my feet like the feet of a deer, He enables me to go on the heights. (Habakkuk 3:17-19)*

Many doubted. But in each case, something wonderful happened - God showed up! They found themselves searching for faith and in the process, they found God!

If truth be told, we would all have to put our hands up and admit that there have been moments in our lives when our faith has been less than it should have been. We all have moments in life, particularly in difficult circumstances, where we don't always understand why things happen the way they do. This was such a moment for Thomas.

Ironically, it was the very encounter with crisis that led to an encounter with Christ!

The Meeting

One week later, just seven days after having appeared to the disciples, Jesus took the time to appear to Thomas! Jesus, in His resurrected beauty, His unlimited power, stood before a broken man. And His first words were identical to the ones He spoke seven days before. God Almighty, the One who alone has the ability and authority to forgive or to condemn, to pardon or to judge, spoke and said to Thomas, "*Peace* be with you."

Even though Thomas had been ravaged by doubt, Jesus came speaking peace! He came to meet Thomas at his very point of need. Thomas would not believe unless he saw for himself, touched Jesus for himself, and so Jesus, in His grace, invited Thomas to do just that! It is my firm conviction that the whole point of this encounter was not to rebuke Thomas, but to restore him. That is the heart of God!

And how did Thomas respond? It would prove to be a life-changing moment for him. Standing in the presence of Christ, the shackles of doubt were broken, the shadows of disillusionment dissolved, and with the faith that would carry him for the next forty years of his life, Thomas exclaimed, "My Lord and my God!"

Later, four decades later to be precise, the same man who wanted to see for himself so that he might believe, became a martyr. Forty years later and Thomas still exclaimed, "My Lord and my God!"

Opening Locked Doors

Now I don't know if you noticed this, but on both occasions that Jesus appeared to His disciples, the doors were locked. Why? One could understand the doors being locked the first time – but why the second as well?

Note too that the doors had been locked from the *inside*. The disciples were not being held as prisoners. Yet, in a way, they were prisoners. Is it possible that some of them, though relieved to have seen Jesus, were still living with a sense of guilt, shame, fear even?

Whether or not it is true of them, I don't know, but I do know that it is true of some Christians today. I have no doubt that some of us still live behind the locked doors of our past even after having met with Jesus – doors locked, not from the outside, but from the inside. Some of us still live under the labels we have been given by others, or labels we have chosen to give ourselves, trapped by the failures, hurts and disappointments of the past.

But just as Jesus took the time to visit Thomas, so He is willing to come to us – as many times as it takes - until we are in a place where we can unlock the door, not to let Him in, but to let ourselves out! His word to you today is the same as His word to Thomas: "Peace!"

Is it time for you to be freed from the label you have worn? Is it time for you to discover a new hope and a future?

Because He lives, hope lives! May God meet with you afresh today - or as many times as it takes for you to be able to say with new-found freedom what Thomas and millions of others have come to say: "My Lord and my God!"

4

Choosing Our Words Well

Text: Mt 4:1-4

Then Jesus was led by the Spirit into the desert to be tempted by the devil. After fasting forty days and forty nights, he was hungry. The tempter came to him and said, "If you are the Son of God, tell these stones to become bread."

Jesus answered, "It is written: 'Man does not live on bread alone, but on every word that comes from the mouth of God'."

Immediately after Jesus was baptised, He was led by the Holy Spirit into the wilderness to be tempted by the devil. After forty days, the tempter came to Him saying, "If You are the Son of God then tell these stones to become bread."

Did you notice that the first temptation involved the tempter using *words* and involved trying to get Jesus to *say* something? I believe that this is quite significant. The Lord's response is equally interesting. He used words to put the tempter in his place and in the process revealed that our spiritual sustenance depends on the Word of God. Quoting from the book of

Deuteronomy, Jesus replied; "It is written: Man does not live by bread alone but on every word that comes from the mouth of God."

Words are clearly important. They wield much power.

> *The tongue has the power of life and death, and those who love it will eat its fruit. (Proverbs 18:21)*

Words can be used for great good, yet also have the corresponding ability to destroy. They can be used as powerful instruments or as catastrophic weapons. As Washington Irving put it:

> "A sharp tongue is the only edged tool that grows keener with constant use."

Publius recognised the potency of words when he said,

> "I have often regretted my speech, but never my silence."

God the Word and the Word of God

God understands the power of words which is very possibly why He inspired John to begin his gospel account describing Jesus as the '*Logos*', the '*Word*' made flesh:

> *In the beginning was the Word, and the Word was with God, and the Word was God...The Word became flesh and made His dwelling among us. (John 1:1, 14)*

The psalmist reminds us of the life-changing benefits of the Word of God:

> *Your word is a lamp to my feet and a light to my path. (Psalm 119:105)*

Words Take Many Forms

Let us consider just how significant words are:

Repentance involves *confessing* our transgressions to God:

> *Take words with you and return to the LORD. Say to him: "Forgive all our sins and receive us graciously, that we may offer the fruit of our lips. (Hosea 14:2)*

> *"If we confess our sins, he is faithful and just and will forgive our sins and purify us from all unrighteousness. (1 John 1:9)*

The professing of our faith involves words:

> *That if you confess with your mouth, "Jesus is Lord," and believe in your heart that God raised him from the dead, you will be saved. (Romans 10:9)*

Passing judgement involves words. Jesus warned us that we will give an account for every idle word we speak:

> *"But I tell you that men will have to give account on the day of judgement for every careless word they have spoken. For by your words you will be acquitted, and by your words you will be condemned."(Matthew 12:36-37)*

Prayer involves words. God invites us to come to Him in prayer, *asking*, seeking and knocking.

Of the seven things God hates, as recorded in Prov 6:16-19, three involve the use of words; a lying tongue, bearing false witness and stirring up dissension between brothers. God clearly places a premium on the use of words.

Furthermore, He instructs us to ensure that our words line up with our walk:

> *Above all, my brothers, do not swear - not by heaven or by earth or by anything else. Let your "Yes" be yes, and your "No," no, or you will be condemned. (James 5:12)*

Weigh Your Words Well

It is thus not surprising to learn that God counsels us to choose our words carefully:

> *My dear brothers, take note of this: Everyone should be quick to listen, slow to speak and slow to become angry. (James 1:19)*

The epistle of James gives a detailed description of the power of the tongue, reminding us to use our words well and to choose our words wisely. The problem of course, is not the mouth so much as the heart:

For out of the overflow of the heart the mouth speaks. (Matthew 12:34b)

If we have a 'mouth' issue, it belies an underlying 'heart' issue. Deal with the heart and you deal with the mouth!

The Power of an Encouraging Word

Since words yield such tremendous power, let us purpose to use our words well, ensuring that what we have to say serves as a source of blessing and encouragement. Barnabas provides a wonderful example of the power of an encouraging word. Although Barnabas never wrote an epistle that we know of, the impact of his words still resonate throughout Christendom to this day. It could be argued that if it wasn't for the ministry of Barnabas, the ministries of people like Paul and Mark may not have been as effective as they were.

A Man Known by another Name

The name Barnabas literally means *Son of Encouragement,* a wonderful and fitting description of the man. However, his real name was Joseph (see Acts 4:36). Barnabas was the affectionate nickname that the apostles gave to him in recognition of his inordinate ability to see potential in people even when others often saw problems. Barnabas was in every sense of the word, a great encourager. He lauded where others judged. He saw value where others found fault. He befriended people when others wanted to wash their hands of them.

Barnabas was the very person who encouraged the early church to embrace Paul at a time when his conversion was viewed with much scepticism and suspicion. The 'Son of Encouragement' broke down the barriers that kept Paul at an arm's length:

> *When he came to Jerusalem, he tried to join the disciples, but they were all afraid of him, not believing that he really was a disciple. But Barnabas took him and brought him to the apostles. He told them how Saul on his journey had seen the Lord and that the Lord had spoken to him, and how in Damascus he had preached fearlessly in the name of Jesus. (Acts 9:26-27)*

The ministry of Paul, as we know, would have a profound impact on the life of the Church. But this was not the only occasion where the actions of Barnabas would benefit Paul. He was also instrumental in launching Paul's missionary ministry to the Gentiles. After Paul's conversion, some Jewish believers fled to Antioch. It was common practice for early Christians to share their faith wherever they went. Up to this point, however, those who had been scattered shared the gospel message exclusively with fellow Jews (it hadn't yet occurred to the early church that God's message of grace through faith in Jesus was available to all, Jew and Gentile alike).

This would change, of course. On settling in Antioch, the Jewish believers began to share the good news with the Greeks, and because God's hand was with them, a great number believed and turned to the Lord. This was both unexpected and unprecedented! Indeed, when news reached the apostles in Jerusalem, they decided to send someone to investigate. Who did they send? Barnabas! Luke records what happened next:

> *When he arrived and saw the evidence of the grace of God, he was glad and encouraged them all to remain true to the Lord with all their hearts. He was a good man, full of the Holy Spirit and faith, and a great number of people were brought to the Lord. (Acts 11:23-24)*

But Barnabas was not solely concerned with encouraging the new believers. He knew that they needed to be effectively discipled, and, given their Gentile heritage, he knew just the man for the job!

Although Paul was a Jew, his upbringing as a Roman citizen would have prepared him to be able to minister in this unique Jewish-Gentile context. And so Barnabas journeyed all the way to Tarsus to fetch Paul:

> *Then Barnabas went to Tarsus to look for Saul, and when he found him, he brought him to Antioch. So for a whole year Barnabas and Saul met with the church and taught great numbers of people. The disciples were called Christians first at Antioch. (Acts 11:25-26)*

A New Name for the Followers of 'The Way'

Barnabas' influence would have a much wider impact, of course. Believers were first called Christians at Antioch. Before this they were known largely as followers of 'The Way'. But upon seeing the incredible transformation in the lives of those who had chosen to follow Christ, people began to identify believers by the very name of their Messiah! Barnabas (and those he touched) made a difference!

Barnabas and Mark

What Barnabas did for Paul, he did for others as well. As you know, there are four gospel accounts in Scripture. The second account is written by a man called Mark (or John Mark as he is sometimes known).

Mark had been invited to assist Barnabas and Paul as they set out on the first ever missionary journey. They set sail, going first to Cyprus and then to Pamphylia. All seemed to be proceeding well. But Luke tells us that Mark left them and returned to Jerusalem.

Although Luke spares us the details here (saying simply that Mark left), we learn in a subsequent account that Mark had actually deserted them (see Acts 15:36-38). For reasons we do not know, Mark found the going too tough and simply abandoned Paul and Barnabas. Returning to the comfort and familiarity of home, Mark left Paul and Barnabas to complete the journey on their own.

Some time later, Paul and Barnabas decided to retrace their steps, wanting to encourage the churches that had been established on their first journey. Barnabas, being the great encourager that he was, saw this as a wonderful opportunity for Mark to be given a second chance, to prove to others that he was the faithful young man Barnabas believed him to be.

Paul was far less optimistic, however. He thought this proposal to be unwise at best – after all, they needed *helpers*, and clearly helpers needed to *be* there! No, if they were going to take a helper along, someone like Silas would be a far better choice.

But Barnabas wasn't about to give up on Mark. He insisted that Mark be given another chance to prove his mettle. They had such a sharp disagreement over the matter that they parted company - Paul took Silas along with him - and Barnabas? Well, he chose Mark, of course!

> *Some time later Paul said to Barnabas, "Let us go back and visit the brothers in all the towns where we preached the word of the Lord and see how they are doing." Barnabas wanted to take John, also called Mark, with them, but Paul did not think it wise to take him, because he had deserted them in Pamphylia and had not continued with them in the work. They had such a sharp disagreement that they parted company. Barnabas took Mark and sailed for Cyprus, but Paul chose Silas and left, commended by the brothers to the grace of the Lord. He went through Syria and Cilicia, strengthening the churches. (Acts 15:36-41)*

Barnabas Stood Up

Barnabas stood up for Paul when no-one else would. He spoke up for Mark when no-one else dared. He kept his tongue during times of criticism. Barnabas chose his words well!

His encouragement would prove to have a life-changing impact on Mark who would become a great asset to the Church. Inspired by the Holy Spirit, Mark would author one of only four universally recognised Gospel account - all because Barnabas stood up to be counted!

Incidentally, Paul later acknowledged that Barnabas was right to have stood by Mark. Writing his second letter to Timothy while in prison (and suffering for his faith), Paul reports that Demas, the man who was supposed to be helping him, had abandoned him. Paul needed help. He needed someone he knew he could rely on. And so he wrote:

> *...Get Mark and bring him with you, because he is helpful to me in my ministry. (2 Timothy 4:11b)*

When the chips were down, Paul needed someone he knew he could count on. And so he asked for Mark! *That* very act reveals the power that an encouraging word can have!

Your Words Make a Difference

Let us take one last moment to reflect on our opening text. As we discovered, the very first temptation Jesus faced was a temptation to *say* something.

Is it possible that this very temptation had been designed to deliberately derail His ministry? I believe it was. Was it a mere coincidence that it involved words? No, I don't believe so.

There is a lesson to be learnt here: Let us not allow ourselves to be robbed of the opportunity to impact the lives of those around us because of the looseness of our tongues. Let us be people who choose our words with great care, ensuring that we have a positive, lasting impact on those we meet along life's journey.

Let us choose our words mindful of the fact that God is listening to what we have to say!

I am told that a tombstone in one of the windswept churchyards in Britain bears a rather unusual epitaph. It reads:

"Beneath this stone, a lump of clay,
Lies Marabella Young
Who, on the twenty-fifth of May,
Began to hold her tongue."

Oh how I pray that we, like Barnabas, would choose to leave an enduring legacy behind - one which reveals the wonderful, life-changing influence our words have had on others. Let us determine to choose our words well, and to use our words wisely.

William Norris sums it up best:

If your lips would keep from slips,
Five things observe with care:
To whom you speak; of whom you speak;
And how, and when, and where.

5

David's Discouragement

Text: 1 Sam 30:1-19

David and his men reached Ziklag on the third day. Now the Amalekites had raided the Negev and Ziklag. They had attacked Ziklag and burned it, and had taken captive the women and all who were in it, both young and old. They killed none of them, but carried them off as they went on their way.

When David and his men came to Ziklag, they found it destroyed by fire and their wives and sons and daughters taken captive. So David and his men wept aloud until they had no strength left to weep. David's two wives had been captured—Ahinoam of Jezreel and Abigail, the widow of Nabal of Carmel. David was greatly distressed because the men were talking of stoning him; each one was bitter in spirit because of his sons and daughters. But David found strength in the LORD his God.

Then David said to Abiathar the priest, the son of Ahimelech, "Bring me the ephod." Abiathar brought it to him, and David inquired of the LORD, "Shall I pursue this raiding party? Will I overtake them?"

"Pursue them," he answered. "You will certainly overtake them and succeed in the rescue."

David and the six hundred men with him came to the Besor Ravine, where some stayed behind, for two hundred men were too exhausted to cross the ravine. But David and four hundred men continued the pursuit.

They found an Egyptian in a field and brought him to David. They gave him water to drink and food to eat - part of a cake of pressed figs and two cakes of raisins. He ate and was revived, for he had not eaten any food or drunk any water for three days and three nights.

David asked him, "To whom do you belong, and where do you come from?"

He said, "I am an Egyptian, the slave of an Amalekite. My master abandoned me when I became ill three days ago. We raided the Negev of the Kerethites and the territory belonging to Judah and the Negev of Caleb. And we burned Ziklag."

David asked him, "Can you lead me down to this raiding party?" He answered, "Swear to me before God that you will not kill me or hand me over to my master, and I will take you down to them."

He led David down, and there they were, scattered over the countryside, eating, drinking and reveling because of the great amount of plunder they had taken from the land of the Philistines and from Judah. David fought them from dusk until the evening of the next day, and none of them got away, except four hundred young men who rode off on camels and fled. David recovered everything the Amalekites had taken, including his two wives. Nothing was missing: young or old, boy or girl, plunder or anything else they had taken. David brought everything back.

But David found strength in the Lord His God. What a remarkable verse! It would be remarkable had this verse applied to any period in David's life, but the fact it is attributed to this moment in time is truly inspiring! Let me explain.

The chapter opens with the account of David and his men returning home to Ziklag only to find that the Amalekites had plundered it in their absence, taking all their women and children captive in the process.

Overcome with despair, David and his men wept until they have no strength left to weep. If ever you have wept that way, you will understand the very depths of despair in which they found themselves. To add insult to injury, David, being the leader, became the target of the soldier's anguish and anger, so much so, in fact, that they even spoke of stoning him. The blame for their plight was being laid squarely at his feet. Consequently, he was greatly distressed. But David, we are told, found strength in the Lord his God.

It is truly inspiring to read an account of how David's faith soared in spite of great personal anguish, danger and distress. One would be forgiven for thinking that David always displayed such unwavering faith and courage, but it might surprise you to learn that this great moment of faith came hot on the heels of a period in David's life where he didn't exactly display much faith in the Lord at all! The fact that David found strength in the Lord his God is of far greater significance than we first realise.

In the Wrong Place at the Wrong Time

All was not as it should have been at this point in David's life. In fact it is fair to say that David was not where he should have been. For the sixteen months preceding this event, David had sojourned in the land of the Philistines.

Having suffered years of oppression at the hand of King Saul whose relentless pursuit was fuelled by jealous rage, David finally fled to the land of the Philistines, setting up camp in Ziklag, a city just across from the border of Israel.

The name Ziklag literally means, "*Measure pressed down*."[6] As the name suggests, it marked a time in David's life where oppression and hardship became familiar, uninvited bedfellows.

What is more, Ziklag was part of a region governed by the king of Gath. Does that name ring a bell? It should. A certain infamous Philistine soldier was from that very part of the world. He was none other than Goliath!

So here is David, the great servant of God, one who has already been anointed by God as King in Saul's place, a young man who had displayed unparalleled faith and exemplary courage when confronting Goliath, now living in the very land of his former nemesis! Why? Had God sent him on some brave errand? No. Was he there by the Lord's leading? No. Was he on a secret mission to overthrow his enemies? No. To the contrary, this great warrior-king who had displayed remarkable courage time and time again, who singlehandedly defended the honour of God and the reputation of a nation against Goliath, who faced down the lion and the bear and prevailed, who boldly proclaimed with heartfelt conviction that God would spare his life from the hand of Saul on two separate occasions - this great man of God was in Ziklag, not because he had such great faith in God, but precisely because he had *lost* faith in God's ability to save him! Even though God had promised David success, years of being hunted had taken their toll:

> *But David thought to himself, "One of these days I will be destroyed by the hand of Saul. The best thing I can do is to escape to the land of the Philistines. Then Saul will give up searching for me anywhere in Israel, and I will slip out of his hand. (1 Samuel 27:1)*

David's Discouragement

In short, David's faith had failed him. Despite God's promise to protect him and despite having already been anointed as King by Samuel, David fled to the very land of his enemies for fear of being destroyed by Saul. Eight years of running had wearied him. David's courage had all but evaporated. He had become *dis*couraged!

David lost sight of the Lord his God. Was God truly with him? Was he really king in God's eyes, or did Samuel get it wrong? Doubt caused him to defect, right into the camp of his former enemy!

1 Samuel 27 is a simple account of David fleeing to the land of the Philistines. It is the story of a young man clearly caught in a crisis of faith. Indeed, the name of God is not mentioned once in the whole of the chapter. There is no record of David calling on God at all in the sixteen months that followed – no record, that is, until the very moment David's men threatened to stone him.

Now it would be easy to turn our noses up at David for his lack of faith, but take a moment to put yourself in his shoes. A demoralised, dejected man finds himself in enemy territory having fled for his life. He has traded the familiarity of his home for the unfamiliar domain of his arch enemies. Even though he has twice spared Saul's life (and even though Saul has twice vowed not to pursue him any more), David finds himself on the run yet again. Compassion had been met with contention. Generosity had been silenced by jealousy, and as a consequence, bewilderment gives way to discouragement. And then, just when it seemed as if things could get no worse, Ziklag, the very place David had now called home, was raided, and all its inhabitants taken captive.

Discouragement turned to grief. Tears flowed - and then ceased - as the very strength to cry was spent. Grief turned to anger. Anger gave way to blame. Here, in the land of the enemy, the great hero was in danger of becoming the hunted once more as his loyal followers, his brothers in arms, began to bay for his blood. Then, just when it seemed utterly hopeless, when it looked like the end had finally come, something wonderful occurred - David found strength in the Lord his God!

The Defeat of Defection

Of course, David would not find safety in the land of his enemy. How could he? God had not led him there. It may have seemed like a good plan, but it nearly ended tragically.

Saul had stopped his pursuit – that part of the plan had worked - but defection did not bring the peace David so longed for. Why? Because David had chosen to rely on his own devices. In order to appease the Philistine rulers (yet not compromise his deep-rooted patriotism), David resorted to deceptive, devious behaviour. As 'payoff' for allowing him to live in the land, David had to show allegiance to his new master, King Achish, by going on raids, plundering villages and sacking homes in order to be able to pay tribute to him. David would soon discover, however, that compromise costs.

To add to his dilemma, David would learn that his Philistine lords wanted him to raid the Israelites. Living in the land of the enemy meant siding with the enemy. However, David could not bring himself to attack his own countrymen and so he schemed and connived as best he could. If he could raid neutral territories (as well as the common enemies of the Israelites and the Philistines) and pretend to be raiding Israel, he could secure the spoils of battle, yet continue the ruse.

This may have helped to appease his conscience to a degree, but it presented him with a dilemma. David would have to cover his tracks. Nobody could know what he was doing, or the game would be up. So, in order to protect his deception, David was forced to sack and destroy every town and village he raided, leaving no witnesses alive to report what he had done. His compromise came at a great cost to many.

Finally, David's deception caught up with him. He was trapped in the very web he had spun. He raided and plundered, raided and plundered... until he was raided and plundered! His deception had placed his very family and the families of all his fighting soldiers in jeopardy. David's cunning plan had begun to unravel.

> *David was greatly distressed because the men were talking of stoning him; each one was bitter in spirit because of his sons and daughters. (1 Samuel 30:6a)*

God Did Not Lose Sight of David

Praise God that the story does not end there! David may have become discouraged and distressed, he may have lost sight of God for a brief moment, but God had not lost sight of David! He might have stopped believing in God, but God had not stopped believing in him! And so, after a year and a half of silence, David finally called on the Lord his God. And the very moment he did, God answered! Praise God for His unmerited favour!

David's Deliverance

David found strength in the Lord, looking to Him for direction once more. And the same God who had protected David against the lion and the bear, who had given him a famous victory against Goliath, who had spared him for eight years from the mad, irrational pursuits of Saul, told him to pursue his attackers. He promised David that he would be victorious. So, with just four hundred exhausted men, David gave chase and won a splendid victory, bringing back alive every wife, every child, every animal - and all the treasure that had been taken.

> *David recovered everything the Amalekites had taken, including his two wives. Nothing was missing: young or old, boy or girl, plunder or anything else they had taken. David brought everything back. He took all the flocks and herds, and his men drove them ahead of the other livestock, saying, "This is David's plunder." (1 Samuel 30:18-20)*

Unbroken by the Storms that Break

There are some invaluable lessons to be learnt of course. Firstly we need to be aware that none are beyond the ravages of doubt and discouragement. If great heroes of the faith like David could experience moments of absolute brokenness, then we are certainly not immune! Storms will visit us, that is certain. Christianity is no insurance against the trials and tribulations of life. Jesus has promised to be with us always, but He hasn't promised us a bed of roses. Any doctrine that precludes suffering from the will of God has misinterpreted Scripture. Suffering, after all, is something God uses to great effect in our lives (see Rom 5:3-5). In fact, He has promised that hardship and heartache will visit us:

> *"I have told you these things, so that in me you may have peace. In this world you will have trouble. But take heart! I have overcome the world." (John 16:33)*

He gives us the assurance, however, that He has overcome the world and will neither leave us nor forsake us. Oh that we would remember to look to Him in times of distress rather than simply try to work things out ourselves.

Like David, there may be times when we think praying makes no difference. For years David was pursued by Saul. For years he prayed for deliverance. There will be times when we, like David, will be tempted to take matters into our own hands rather than look to God. But throwing up our hands in defeat is no substitute for lifting up our hands in prayer! Indeed, we need to be people of persistent prayer. God may not answer as we expect or when we anticipate, but He will answer!

Storms will break, but we need not be broken by them. David's willingness to trust God despite the difficulties he faced is a wonderful testimony that brings much glory to God. It may be that God calls us to face storms that do not relent soon - or even in our lifetime. If this is so, we will not be the first. In the great chapter of faith heroes, Hebrews 11, God reserves for last the account of people whose prayers were not answered in their lifetimes. They never received what was promised to them. Yet they never stopped trusting in God. Their faith remained steadfast, unwavering, unbowed! They may not have seen great miracles as a consequence of their faith as others had done. They did not experience the parting of the sea or the raising of the dead, but despite this, the greatest honour is reserved for them. The author of Hebrews simply says, "The world was not worthy of them."

> *Women received back their dead, raised to life again. Others were tortured and refused to be released, so that they might gain a better resurrection. Some faced jeers and flogging, while still others were chained and put in prison. They were stoned; they were sawed in two; they were put to death by the sword. They went about in sheepskins and goatskins, destitute, persecuted and mistreated — the world was not worthy of them. They wandered in deserts and mountains, and in caves and holes in the ground. These were all commended for their faith, yet none of them received what had been promised. (Hebrews 11:35-39)*

That is faith! Such is a life that brings glory to God! Storms will come. Storms will break. But we need not be broken by them!

Today's Decisions Impact Tomorrow's Journey...

David lost sight of the Lord for one brief moment. In fact, had God not intervened, things could have gone horribly wrong. We learn from David that the very real temptation in times of discouragement and despair is to withdraw from the Lord and to take matters into our own hands. Somehow finding the strength to pray at times like this is difficult, but the only way we can be strengthened *is* in the Lord our God!

Hard times are the very times when we need to pray more earnestly than ever. David made a decision in a time of discouragement outside of the Lord's leading - and suffered the consequences. It serves as a sober reminder that today's decisions impact tomorrow's journey. Let us make sure that we look to the Lord at all times - especially during times when we are discouraged.

... But Tomorrow's Outcome is Not Inevitable

When we become discouraged, the temptation will be to draw very negative conclusions about what tomorrow holds. By nature we tend to paint the worst possible picture; "I failed, therefore God can't use me again!" or, "I've taken a wrong turn, therefore I've blown any chance of being in God's perfect will. I'll have to settle for His permissive will instead!"

That might be your perception, but thankfully, it is not His! I find it so encouraging to know that God never removed his hand from David even though David removed his gaze from God. The Lord was still able to weave His will through the tapestry of David's life despite the poor choices David made and despite his many shortfalls. One of the most amazing attributes of God is His sovereign ability to accomplish His will in spite of our poor choices and errors of judgement.

In His infinite wisdom, God can work all things together for good to all who love Him and are called according to His purpose. While today's decisions impact tomorrow's journey, God in His grace, is able to write a new chapter in our lives. It all begins when we turn to Him once more. Is it time to strengthen yourself in the Lord your God?

Tomorrow's Heroes are not necessarily Today's Champions

David's example teaches us that God remains fully God even when we experience moments of weakness. Even though we might give up on God (or on ourselves) He will not give up on us.

God doesn't paint unrealistic pictures of His heroes. He reveals them to us warts and all because their accomplishments are ultimately a consequence of His grace, not their abilities.

God doesn't place people on pedestals or pretend that they are perfect saints with shiny halos. Abraham lied. Noah got drunk. Moses lost his temper and committed murder. Rahab was a harlot. David committed murder and adultery. Yet they are listed in Hebrews 11 as heroes of the faith. God was able to use them in incredible ways precisely because they chose to put their trust in Him. Their moral shortfalls did not mark the end of their journey with God or their usefulness to Him. He corrected where correction was needed. He disciplined when discipline was necessary. But God never washed His hands of any of them! Let us take comfort in the fact that God is not ashamed to put His treasure in vessels of clay!

Today's Mistakes May Very Well be the Means by Which God Fulfils Yesterday's Promises

Finally, David's life teaches us that God is able to use today's mistakes to fulfil yesterday's promises. What do I mean? As we have seen, David camped at Ziklag, not because God told him to, but because he lost faith. Yet Ziklag was part of God's promised inheritance to Israel. In Joshua 15:31 & 19:5 we read that God had promised Ziklag as an allotment both to the tribes of Judah and Simeon and to the kings of Israel.

Even in the midst of this dark, doubt-filled moment in David's life, one brought about undeniably of his own choosing in many respects, God was able to fulfil a promise to the Israelites: Ziklag would become part of Israel's territory from this very time on! God truly is able to work all things together for good to those who love Him and are called according to His purposes - even our failures!

In His sovereign, omniscient omnipotence, God is able to take every storm, every circumstance, every injury, every attack, every failure, every compromise, every hardship, every heartache and make something good come out of it. Let us put our trust in Him. Let us strengthen ourselves in Him once more! We may just be amazed by what He is able to do!

6

Peter Restored

Text: John 21:1-19

Afterward Jesus appeared again to his disciples, by the Sea of Tiberias. It happened this way: Simon Peter, Thomas (called Didymus), Nathanael from Cana in Galilee, the sons of Zebedee, and two other disciples were together. "I'm going out to fish," Simon Peter told them, and they said, "We'll go with you." So they went out and got into the boat, but that night they caught nothing.

Early in the morning, Jesus stood on the shore, but the disciples did not realize that it was Jesus.

He called out to them, "Friends, haven't you any fish?" "No," they answered.

He said, "Throw your net on the right side of the boat and you will find some." When they did, they were unable to haul the net in because of the large number of fish.

Then the disciple whom Jesus loved said to Peter, "It is the Lord!" As soon as Simon Peter heard him say, "It is the Lord," he wrapped his outer garment around him (for he had taken it off) and jumped into the water. The other disciples followed in the boat, towing the net full of fish, for they were not far from shore, about a hundred yards. When they landed, they saw a fire of burning coals there with fish on it, and some bread.

Jesus said to them, "Bring some of the fish you have just caught."

Simon Peter climbed aboard and dragged the net ashore. It was full of large fish, 153, but even with so many the net was not torn. Jesus said to them, "Come and have breakfast." None of the disciples dared ask him, "Who are you?" They knew it was the Lord. Jesus came, took the bread and gave it to them, and did the same with the fish. This was now the third time Jesus appeared to his disciples after he was raised from the dead.

When they had finished eating, Jesus said to Simon Peter, "Simon son of John, do you truly love me more than these?"
"Yes, Lord," he said, "you know that I love you."
Jesus said, "Feed my lambs."

Again Jesus said, "Simon son of John, do you truly love me?"
He answered, "Yes, Lord, you know that I love you."
Jesus said, "Take care of my sheep."

The third time he said to him, "Simon son of John, do you love me?"
Peter was hurt because Jesus asked him the third time, "Do you love me?" He said, "Lord, you know all things; you know that I love you."

Jesus said, "Feed my sheep. I tell you the truth, when you were younger you dressed yourself and went where you wanted; but when you are old you will stretch out your hands, and someone else will dress you and lead you where you do not want to go." Jesus said this to indicate the kind of death by which Peter would glorify God. Then he said to him, "Follow me!"

As the sun rose over the horizon, the eyes of the disciples scanned the shoreline. They saw a man preparing breakfast over an open fire; a familiar figure perhaps? They could not say at this distance. What they did know, however, was that they weren't meant to be there...

The Disciples Were Not Where They Were Meant to Be

Jesus had given His disciples very specific instructions on two separate occasions about where they were to meet Him after His resurrection. In the first instance, Jesus spoke to them personally:

> *But after I have risen, I will go ahead of you into Galilee." Peter declared, "Even if all fall away, I will not."*
>
> *"I tell you the truth," Jesus answered, "today—yes, tonight—before the rooster crows twice you yourself will disown me three times."*
>
> *But Peter insisted emphatically, "Even if I have to die with you, I will never disown you." And all the others said the same. (Mark 14:28-31)*

In the second instance, the angels told the ladies to tell the disciples where they were to meet Him:

> *When the Sabbath was over, Mary Magdalene, Mary the mother of James, and Salome bought spices so that they might go to anoint Jesus' body. Very early on the first day of the week, just after sunrise, they were on their way to the tomb and they asked each other, "Who will roll the stone away from the entrance of the tomb?"*
>
> *But when they looked up, they saw that the stone, which was very large, had been rolled away. As they entered the tomb, they*

saw a young man dressed in a white robe sitting on the right side, and they were alarmed.

"Don't be alarmed," he said. "You are looking for Jesus the Nazarene, who was crucified. He has risen! He is not here. See the place where they laid him. But go, tell his disciples and Peter, 'He is going ahead of you into Galilee. There you will see him, just as he told you.'" (Mark 16:1-7)

Not only were the disciples to go to Galilee to meet Jesus after His resurrection, but Matthew records that they were told to go to a very specific place in Galilee:

Then the eleven disciples went to Galilee, to the mountain where Jesus had told them to go. (Matthew 28:16)

So the disciples were meant to go to Galilee to meet Jesus on a specific mountain.

But where were they when they first met Jesus in Galilee? They were fishing close to the shore of the Sea of Tiberius. The disciples were not where they were meant to be.

They Were Not Doing What They Were Meant to be Doing

The disciples were meant to be meeting with Jesus on the mountain. Instead they were fishing on the Sea of Tiberius. Why? Some could argue that they were hungry and had stopped on the way to catch some fish so that they could eat. However, a quick study of the topography would reveal that Tiberius lay beyond the Galilean mountains.

Tiberius is a coastal town in Galilee, north-east of Jerusalem. The sea surrounding the town is referred to as the Sea of Tiberius and is part of a larger body of water called the Sea of Galilee. The whole western shore is lined by a mountain range, which means that in order to get to the Sea of Tiberius from Jerusalem one would have to cross over the mountains first!

In other words, it was not a case of stopping off for a bite to eat *en route* to the mountain in Galilee. Instead, the disciples had already been on the mountain in Galilee and had subsequently decided to travel down the other side.

Peter's suggestion that they go fishing (and the fact that seven of the disciples decided to accompany him) suggests far more than a practical detour – much more than that in fact!

Prior to His crucifixion, Jesus told His disciples that they would all desert Him. He mentioned that Peter would deny Him three times. However, once He had risen, He promised to go *ahead* of them and meet them on the mountain in Galilee. Peter was obstinate. How could Jesus question his devotion? He was, after all, willing to die with Christ – not to deny Him! Even if all the other disciples deserted Him, Jesus could count on Peter!

But Peter *had* denied Him, just as Jesus said he would. The disciples *had* deserted Him, just as He foretold.

Then Mary and the women brought word that they had seen Jesus and that they were to meet Him on the mountain in Galilee. He would go *ahead* of them and meet them there.

And so they travelled from Jerusalem to Galilee. They arrived on the mountain ... and Jesus was not there.

Is it possible that Peter's decision to go fishing (remember that he used to be a fisherman by trade) was more than simply a passing whim? You know, I believe it was. He was obviously in a very vulnerable state. Could He have misinterpreted Jesus' absence on the mountain as a sign of rejection?

After all, Peter had been singled out by Jesus: "Go tell the disciples *and* Peter..."

Jesus had seen such potential in Peter – He had even referred to him as the stone (petros) on which He would build His Church. Jesus had such dreams for Peter. And yet this man of promise had done the unthinkable – he had denied His very Saviour - not once, but three times!

Now, in broken, bowed obedience, Peter had dared to dream again. Travelling to Galilee as Jesus had told him to, Peter had made the arduous journey up the mountain. Peter was there. But where was Jesus? Had Jesus changed His mind? Peter knew he deserved no better. Had Jesus snubbed the disciples publicly as a reminder of the fact that they had denied Him publicly? Was it time to give up on the dream of serving Him? Was it time to go back to the fishing trade? I believe that this may very well have been the moment that Peter had given up; not on God, no, but on the dream of ever being used by Him again!

The God of the Mountain is Still God in the Valley

Incidentally, what was the purpose of their going to the mountain? Well, when they do eventually meet Jesus on the mountain in Galilee, He would commission them. It would be the very moment of the Great Commission (see Matthew 28:16-20).

Clearly Jesus had neither given up on Peter nor the disciples. They may have deserted Him, but He was not about to desert them!

In fact, Jesus *had* gone ahead of them - but He had done more than that. Knowing that they would go fishing, Jesus went ahead of them to prepare breakfast!

Before commissioning them, Jesus wanted to restore them. After all, Peter needed to know that his sin would not keep him from Christ the Saviour. Jesus loved Peter enough to commission him. But he loved Peter the *person* above Peter the *servant* - He loved him for who he was, not for what he would do! And so He chose to restore him *before* He chose to commission him.

Peter Restored

I love the way Jesus restored Peter - it trumpets His tender mercies! Firstly, Jesus eats with him.

Restored *Communion*.

I don't know if you've noticed this, but eating together, breaking bread together, is such an important part of God's dealings with us. Even in Old Testament times, people were told to bring sacrifices, primarily of food.

When they remembered significant events and acts of God, what did they do? They held feasts. When Jesus came to earth, what did He do more often than not (which earned him the disfavour of the religious leaders)? He *ate* with people - he *communed* with them.

Jesus ate with sinners and publicans. He asked the Samaritan woman for water and then spoke to her.

When we remember His sacrifice on our behalf, we *eat* at His table. When Jesus returns at the consummation of the age, we will enjoy a wedding feast together with Him. Why is that? Because there is something about sitting together around a meal, isn't there? Eating together builds fellowship; it allows you to get to know the person you are eating with in a social capacity rather than simply an official one. Communion encourages fellowship. Fellowship cultivates friendship. When God came to restore Peter (and the others), He chose to do so over a meal. *He* prepared the food; *He* extended the invitation - All Peter had to do was accept the invitation and come just as he was!

Restored *Communication.*

Next Jesus *conversed* with Peter. But did you notice that Jesus did not bring up the past? Rather, He spoke of the present, and the future.

He started by asking Peter, "*Do* you love Me?" Obviously there was so much Jesus could have said. But Jesus did not mention the past. Why not? Surely God would want to remind us of what we have done if He is going to restore us. But He doesn't. You don't need to remind a broken man that he is broken.

Jesus didn't remind Peter of his failures because He keeps no record of wrongs! It sounds a bit like the time the woman was caught in adultery doesn't it? Jesus simply said to her, "I do not condemn you. Go and sin no more!" Jesus reminded the penitent woman that she had a hope and a future in Him! Hope lives because *He* lives!

The same can be said of the prodigal. The wayward son had a wonderful speech of repentance prepared for his father, but he didn't even get half way through it before the father stopped him.

And what did the father do? Why, he prepared a banquet for him of course!

Restored *Commission.*

Finally, Jesus restored Peter's *commission.* He asked three questions of Peter. Now our first thought is often that Jesus did this in order to remind

Peter that he had denied Him three times. But is there another explanation? I believe there is.

Jesus had no intention of making Peter feel bad enough first before he could be allowed to feel better. In fact, a closer inspection will reveal that the emphasis was not on what Peter had done, but rather on what Peter was going to do. Jesus didn't bring up the past; rather He reminded Peter about what he would do.

Did you notice that Jesus didn't actually ask Peter the same question three times? But He did commission him three times. What do I mean? Let us take a moment to look at the Greek words that Jesus used here. I have placed the Greek words in brackets:

Question 1: Peter, do you love (*agapē*) Me *more than these*?

Question 2: Peter do you love (*agapē*) Me?

Question 3: Peter do you love (*phileō*) Me?

Note that in the first two instances, Jesus asks Peter if he loves (*agapē*) Him. The third time, however, Jesus asks, "Peter, do you (*phileō*) Me?" What did Jesus mean?

The word *agapē* speaks of the unconditional, sacrificial love of God. *Phileō* on the other hand refers to brotherly love. While still a very noble form of love (people are willing to lay down their lives for their kin after all), brotherly love is always a lesser love when compared to the unconditional God-kind of love (*agapē*).

On the other hand, *agapē* is not subject to relationship or family ties. A*gapē* is love without conditions attached – we love unconditionally and unequivocally, not because we are related, but regardless of whether we are or aren't!

Agapē is the very God-kind of love in action! For God *so* loved (*agapē*) the world that he gave His Son so that whosoever believes in Him will not perish but have everlasting life. That is unconditional love (*agapē*)!

And so Jesus asked three separate questions using two very different words to describe love. Firstly Jesus asked: "Peter, do you love (*agapē*) Me unconditionally, *more than these*? Do you love me unconditionally, more than the other disciples do?" Peter could not respond as impetuously as he once had. His actions had belied his words, after all. He had once boasted, "Even if everyone else deserts You, Lord, I won't!"

But he had deserted Christ! He now knew better. And so Peter could simply respond, "Lord, You know that I love *(phileō)* You, You know that I love You as a brother. I cannot claim to love You in the same way You love me. Nor can I claim to love You more than the others."

Jesus then asked the second question; "Peter, do you love (agapē) Me?" This time He didn't ask Peter whether he loved Him more than the others. He didn't need to. Peter knew better.

Peter's reply was the same. "Jesus, you know that I love *(phileō)* you as a brother."

Finally Jesus asked, "Peter *do* you *phileō* Me? *Do* you love me as a brother?"

Jesus asked three different questions of Peter - and lowered the bar on each occasion.

After the third question however, we read that Peter was hurt. Why? Twice Jesus had asked if Peter's love for Him was unconditional, the same kind of love as the love that God has for us. Peter simply responded, "Lord you know I love You as a brother." But on the third occasion, Jesus seemed to be questioning whether Peter was even capable of loving Him as a brother.

Hurt, yet resigned in the knowledge that His omniscient Saviour knew him far better than he knew himself, Peter simply responded, "Lord, You know all things." Was it possible that Jesus knew what Peter failed to see? Was it possible that he didn't even love Jesus as a brother?

Three questions were asked. Three times the bar was lowered. Had Jesus done this to humiliate Peter? No. Was He condemning Peter? No. You see, while he lowered the bar regarding the questions about Peter's love, He *raised* the bar regarding Peter's commission! Let's take a moment to recap. The conversation goes something like this:

"Peter, do you love Me with the same unconditional and sacrificial love with which I love you, a love that is greater than the other disciples here with you?"

"Lord, you know that I love you as a brother, but I cannot claim to love You as You love Me, and certainly not more than the other disciples."

"Feed My *lambs*."

Jesus was saying, "Peter, although you may not love me as I love you, and although you may not love me more than the other disciples, nevertheless I have still called you; I have still commissioned you! You haven't blown it Peter! My grace is sufficient for you! Feed my lambs. Feed those who are young in their faith."

The second question: "Peter, do you love Me as much as I love you?" Peter's response: "I can't claim to love You that way Lord, but I love You as if You were my brother."

"Take care of My *sheep*. Take care of those who are mature in their faith."

The third question: "Peter, *do* you love me as a brother?" Peter's response? "Lord, only You know."

"Feed My sheep. Teach my mature ones."

I believe Jesus asked Peter three distinct questions not because Peter denied Christ three times but because he needed three reminders that God's grace is more than enough!

The Lesson

The lesson for us is not that we have license to sin as we please because we have the assurance of an abundance of grace. No! In fact, the Bible warns against having that kind of attitude. But what we do learn is that our failures do not signal the end of His love for us or of His desire to enable and empower us. The God who is willing to forgive us is also more than able to restore us!

Peter may not have done what he was meant to do. He may not have been where he was meant to be, but God loved him enough to visit him where he was! God came down to Peter's level and lifted him up to new heights! He came to restore communion with him, to invite him back to His table, to restore communication with him, to get him back into a right relationship, and to restore his commission, to get him back to doing what he had been saved and set apart to do.

I believe this to be the reward of every penitent heart. God is willing to run to meet you. That is the heart of God! If you are unable to meet Him on the mountain, He will meet you in the valley. He will prepare a meal for you, commune with you, converse with you and commission you – if you will only let Him.

Be encouraged that a forgiving God has promised not to smother smouldering flax or to break a bruised reed.

When you can stand in the presence of God, as Peter did, knowing that you are not what you thought you were, and not what you hope to be, He will not bring up the record of your wrongs – because as far as He is concerned, they no longer exist! As far as the east is from the west, so far has He removed our transgressions from us!

Do you believe that? Then it is time to realise that your place is at His table! His invitation is open to you today!

7

Friends of Christ

Text: John 15:15

> *I no longer call you servants, because a servant does not know his master's business. Instead, I have called you friends, for everything that I learned from my Father I have made known to you.*

In chapter fifteen of his gospel account, John records Christ's final teaching before His crucifixion. Nearing the end of His earthly ministry, Jesus celebrated the Passover meal with His disciples, reminding them that the time of His departure was at hand. While He had ministered to them for more than three years, now, in the shadow of the cross, so to speak, Jesus would do something for the very first time – He would call them friends.

> *I no longer call you servants, because a servant does not know his master's business. Instead, I have called you friends, for everything that I learned from my Father I have made known to you. (John 15:15)*

Given the occasion, an interesting question springs to mind: When Jesus called the disciples His friends, was Judas present? Did Jesus call Judas, 'friend?' The answer is no. John makes it clear that Jesus had already exposed Judas as the one who would betray him and Judas had already left to carry out his dastardly deed. Judas may have been chosen by Christ, but He was no friend to Christ!

> *Then Jesus replied, "Have I not chosen you, the Twelve? Yet one of you is a devil!" (He meant Judas, the son of Simon Iscariot, who, though one of the Twelve, was later to betray him.) (John 6:70-71)*

Now it would be wonderful to conclude that Judas is an exception to the rule. But a simple reading of Matthew 7:21-23 would suggest that this could just as easily apply to any one of us:

> *"Not everyone who says to me, 'Lord, Lord,' will enter the kingdom of heaven, but only he who does the will of my Father who is in heaven. Many will say to me on that day, 'Lord, Lord, did we not prophesy in your name, and in your name drive out demons and perform many miracles?' Then I will tell them plainly, 'I never knew you. Away from me, you evildoers!' (Matthew 7:21-23)*

It is clear that there were, are and will be people who have been chosen by Christ, who have served, are serving or will serve in His very name, yet who are not referred to by Him as 'friend!'

The 'Pretend Friend'

I don't know about you, but I struggle to get my head around the fact that Judas could have spent three years of his life within an arm's length of Jesus and yet still remain so untouched by Him. Here was a man who would have seen first-hand the incredible miracles which authenticated the Lord's ministry and mission. He would have seen how the demoniac was healed, how the multitude had been fed, how Lazarus was raised from the dead. He would have heard the life-changing teachings of Jesus who taught as no other, leaving people amazed and astounded by His wisdom. He would have heard how Jesus challenged the Pharisees and Sadducees publicly and found them wanting (the very men with whom Judas would conspire to betray Jesus!). Judas lived the final three years of his life within an arm's length of Jesus, yet clearly remained unmoved and unchanged by Him!

Sadly, Judas would use the kiss of a friend as the very sign with which to betray Christ. Sadder still is the solemn revelation that Judas missed out on one of the most important occasions – the very moment Jesus Christ called His disciples, "friends." Judas was, at best, a 'pretend-friend!'

Friendship According to Jesus

The reality is quite sobering; we are not friends of Christ when *we* say we are - we are friends of Christ when *He* says we are! Fortunately, Jesus has clarified how He sees friendship. In the very same chapter of John's gospel, Jesus made it clear what a friend of Christ looks like; what a friend of Christ does:

'You are my friends if you do what I command.'(John 15:14)

Jesus taught His disciples that a friend was someone who obeyed Him. Interestingly, John lists three commands that Jesus gave His disciples in this very context.

Friends of Christ Look like Christ

A brief survey of chapter fifteen reveals that Jesus had just commanded His disciples to do three specific things. Firstly, Jesus commanded them to:

> *Remain in Me and I will remain in you. No branch can bear fruit by itself; it must remain in the vine. Neither can you bear fruit unless you remain in Me. (John 15:4)*

The Greek for 'remain' is μένω (me'-nō), and it means, 'To abide, to continue to be present, to dwell'. Jesus was literally saying, "Continue to be present in Me, and I will continue to be present in you."

We recognise someone as a friend of Christ when we see evidence that Christ is present; we see Jesus in them! A friend of Christ *looks* like Christ. We see Jesus in their eyes. We feel Jesus in their touch.

The disciples proved their obedience to Christ through their very lives – people saw Christ in them. When Peter and John first appeared before the Sanhedrin giving an account of Christ, the council recognised that there was something quite special, quite unique about these men. What was it?

> *When they saw the courage of Peter and John and realized that they were unschooled, ordinary men, they were astonished and they took note that these men had been with Jesus. (Acts 4:13)*

They took note that these men *had been with Jesus*! A friend of Christ *looks* like Christ.

Friends of Christ Love like Christ

Secondly, Jesus, on this very occasion commanded his friends to:

> *Love one another as I have loved you. (John 15:12)*

Jesus didn't simply say, 'Love one another'. He said, 'Love one another *as I have loved you'* and then showed the extent of His love by going out and dying on the cross. Jesus' love is unconditional, sacrificial love, and those who obey Him are called to love one another in the same way.

> *Greater love has no one than this, that he lay down his life for his friends. (John 15:13)*

Jesus meant what He said. When He said, "My friends love one another *as* I love them," He meant it! The disciples would learn to love this way of course. Of the eleven remaining disciples, all but John would be martyred for their faith (John having been exiled to Patmos). The disciples sacrificed their lives for the privilege of telling others about Christ!

Again, we see an example of this kind of love in action in Acts 2 where the believers ensured that everybody in their number was adequately cared for. They sold houses and land and placed the money at the apostle's feet so that nobody among them went without. This was, in every sense of the word, sacrificial love, the very kind of love by which Jesus identified those He called friends!

I have seen too many churches where love is something that is spoken of much, but lived out little. Aren't you hungry for more? Aren't you hungry to see the love of Christ in action as we see in the early Church?

One of the chief objections that people have of Christianity is not Christ, but Christians! They see what we say and how we live and notice a major inconsistency between our profession of faith and our lifestyles. Sadly, on some level they are right.

How tragic it would be to spend the rest of our lives living an arm's length away from Christ yet not allowing ourselves to be changed *by* Him! Friends of Christ *look* like Christ. Friends of Christ *love* like Christ.

The Bible also makes it clear that our love for others is an expression of our love for God. Just as one cannot separate the vertical and horizontal beams of the cross and still have a cross, so we cannot separate the first and second commandments and still call ourselves friends of Christ. We are to love God with all our heart, soul, mind and strength, and the natural outworking of such a love will be a deep desire to love one another as we love ourselves. By this very love will all men know that we *are* disciples of

Christ! Are you a friend of Christ? Do you love this way? Consider what James says:

> *What good is it, my brothers, if a man claims to have faith but has no deeds? Can such faith save him? Suppose a brother or sister is without clothes and daily food. If one of you says to him, "Go, I wish you well; keep warm and well fed," but does nothing about his physical needs, what good is it? In the same way, faith by itself, if it is not accompanied by action, is dead. (James 2:14-17)*

Furthermore, Jesus makes it clear that to love one another *is* to love Him!

> *"Then the King will say to those on his right, 'Come, you who are blessed by my Father; take your inheritance, the kingdom prepared for you since the creation of the world. For I was hungry and you gave me something to eat, I was thirsty and you gave me something to drink, I was a stranger and you invited me in, I needed clothes and you clothed me, I was sick and you looked after me, I was in prison and you came to visit me.'*
>
> *"Then the righteous will answer him, 'Lord, when did we see you hungry and feed you, or thirsty and give you something to drink? When did we see you a stranger and invite you in, or needing clothes and clothe you? When did we see you sick or in prison and go to visit you?'*
>
> *"The King will reply, 'I tell you the truth, whatever you did for one of the least of these brothers of mine, you did for me.' (Matthew 25:34-40)*

Friends of Christ *look* like Christ. Friends of Christ *love* like Christ. But Jesus gave a third command by which His friends would be identified.

Friends of Christ Speak of Christ

> *"When the Counselor comes, whom I will send to you from the Father, the Spirit of truth who goes out from the Father, he will testify about me. And you also must testify, for you have been with me from the beginning." (John 15:26-27)*

Jesus prefaced His third command by telling His disciples that it would cost them greatly to testify about Him. He warned them that they would be persecuted just as He would be. These words must have been fresh in their minds when they saw Jesus on the cross just hours later. Still, Jesus told them that they were to tell others about Him. What is more, He promised to send the Holy Spirit as a helper, empowering them to be able to testify about Him:

> *But you will receive power when the Holy Spirit comes on you; and you will be my witnesses in Jerusalem, and in all Judea and Samaria, and to the ends of the earth." (Acts 1:8)*

When the Holy Spirit is at work, testimony and attention is focused on the life and ministry of Jesus Christ. You can be sure of that! Jesus told His disciples that they too would testify of Him as the Holy Spirit prompted them.

It is not surprising, then, that Peter's first act of ministry was to testify about Christ. Friends of Christ *speak* of Christ! It is the third mark of friendship according to Jesus. I hope that stirs something in your heart!

Incidentally, the Original Greek word for 'testify' is μαρτυρέω (*mär-tü-re'-ō*). It is the root word from which we get our English word 'martyr.' It literally means, 'To affirm that one has seen or heard or experienced something, or that he knows it because it is taught by divine revelation or inspiration; to give (not to keep back) testimony; to utter honourable testimony, to give a good report; to implore.' [7]

Given the criteria Jesus mentioned, can we truly call ourselves friends of Christ?

Jesus, the Friend of Sinners

As people who desire to be known as friends of Christ and not 'pretend-friends,' are we befriending the people Christ befriended? You see, it strikes me that a friend of Christ will not only look like Him, love like Him and speak of Him, but will respond like Him too! Friends share the same interests and values. Jesus was not only a friend to His disciples, but a friend to sinners:

> *For John came neither eating nor drinking, and they say, 'He has a demon.' The Son of Man came eating and drinking, and they say, 'Here is a glutton and a drunkard, a friend of tax collectors and "sinners." 'But wisdom is proved right by her actions."* (Mt 11:18-19)

Are we, like Jesus, intentionally engaging with people who do not know Him because we so desperately want them to know Him? Do we value them as people for whom Christ died or do we allow their sin to cloud our judgement? Are we taking time to forge friendships which afford people an opportunity to hear and see the good news in action? Are we being the friends of Christ to our generation?

How Are We Presenting Christ?

Finally, it doesn't help bearing witness about Jesus if we are presenting the wrong perception of Jesus to the world. It is my firm conviction that we should avoid 'dumbing-down' the gospel message or trying instead to present a 'politically correct' version of Christ in a desire to be relevant. We don't need a slick, polished 'performance-orientated' Saviour. Rather, we need to make Him known *as* He is.

As Joel Edwards puts it, the Church needs to get out of the circus and into the reality of a world in crisis, out of a consumerist mindset and into a place where we recognise that God is missional and calls *us* to be transformed so that we might transform others. [8]

People must be given the opportunity to say 'yes' or to say 'no' to Christ. If we do not take up this challenge, it will not happen. But let us give them an opportunity to make an informed choice. Let us present to them the *real* Jesus! Let us not fall into the trap of,

> "...clothing Him so heavily in our likeness that He becomes discredited in our culture."[9]

Let us not offer people a bad imitation of Christ, but let us be credible witnesses of the *real* Jesus! Joel Edwards concludes:

> "And the real Jesus was always willing to touch the untouchables. He reached out to those of other faiths and cultures. He healed the ones who did not return to thank Him. He allowed a prostitute to wash His feet in public. And when He taught, it was never predictable or moralising. All the people said that they had never heard anything like it before. The real Jesus turned the most ordinary water into the finest of wines." [10]

I have no doubt that God can touch the heart of our nations once more. We may live in post-modern times (some might even suggest we live in post-Christian times). But I am convinced that the gospel is just as vibrant and just as vital today as it has ever been! After all, the health of the Church is not dependant on culture but on Christ.

He will build His Church and the gates of hell will not be able to prevail against it. However, if we are to see the hand of God at work in our day, then we need to accept the challenge to discover afresh what it means to be friends of Christ, longing to be known as people who have been with

Him and have been transformed by Him; people who *look* like Him, *love* like Him and eagerly *tell* others about Him. Would the friends of Christ please stand up!

8

The Boomerang of Bitterness

Text: ***2 Sam 17:23***

When Ahithophel saw that his advice had not been followed, he saddled his donkey and set out for his house in his hometown. He put his house in order and then hanged himself. So he died and was buried in his father's tomb.

Ahithophel seemed to have the world at his feet. Sought after by kings for his wisdom and held in high esteem by his peers, one could be forgiven for thinking that Ahithophel had it all. But his life would end tragically by his own hand, hope hounded, faith faded and peace pulverised - all because of an acrid attitude.

Ahithophel had served faithfully as King David's counsellor:

Ahithophel was the king's counselor. Hushai the Arkite was the king's friend. (1 Chronicles 27:33)

What is more, his counsel was held in high regard by David and Absalom alike. Indeed, as far as they were concerned, listening to Ahithophel's advice was like listening to the very wisdom of God:

> *Now in those days the advice Ahithophel gave was like that of one who inquires of God. That was how both David and Absalom regarded all of Ahithophel's advice. (2 Samuel 16:23)*

Yet at a crucial time in Israel's history when Ahithophel could have (and should have) quelled an uprising, he chose instead to side with Absalom in his rebellious quest to usurp the throne of his father King David.

Fully aware of Absalom's devious plans, Ahithophel encouraged him to goad his father into conflict by sleeping with his concubines on the very roof of the palace and to do so in broad daylight. Absalom obeyed.

He then counselled Absalom to pursue and attack David before he had a chance to organise an army to defend himself. Knowing that David was arguably the most skilled warrior of his time, Ahithophel knew that any delay would play directly into David's hands.

Ahithophel also knew that by advising Absalom, he had become complicit in his rebellion. He had nailed his colours to the mast. There would be no going back now. Indeed, his very future depended on Absalom's success.

But God was with David. He had determined to frustrate the good advice of Ahithophel in order to bring disaster upon Absalom. Subsequently Absalom sought the counsel of Hushai the Arkite, who advised him not to listen to Ahithophel in pursuing David speedily, but rather to summon men from Dan to Beersheba to come to his aid in battle.

Ahithophel knew that to delay would lead to certain failure. So, when it became evident that Absolom would follow Hushai's advice instead, Ahithophel came to the sobering realisation that his fate was all but sealed. He saddled his donkey, set out for his hometown, put his house in order and hanged himself. History records that Absalom's ruse failed. David would still be king.

Now the big question is, "Why?" What motivated Ahithophel to betray David and side with Absalom in the first place? Did he stand to gain a more prestigious position? No. As a matter of fact, he was taking a very dangerous gamble, trading a very secure position for a risky one at best.

Neither position nor wealth motivated him. Why then, after years of faithful service, would Ahithophel turn against David? To find the answer, we have to dig a little deeper.

2 Sam 23:34 lists David's mighty men. We are told that one of these mighty men was Eliam, the son of Ahithophel. Now Eliam had a daughter, and her name was... Bathsheba!

> *One evening David got up from his bed and walked around on the roof of the palace. From the roof he saw a woman bathing. The woman was very beautiful, and David sent someone to find out about her. The man said, "Isn't this Bathsheba, the daughter of Eliam and the wife of Uriah the Hittite?" (2 Samuel 11:2)*

So, Bathsheba was the daughter of Eliam, the son of Ahithophel. In other words, Bathsheba was Ahithophel's granddaughter!

Bathsheba had been stolen away by David, and Uriah her husband had been murdered. It was a terrible injustice.

In time God forgave David, but clearly, Ahithophel did not! He harboured a grudge against David that lasted for several years. It festered in his heart, fuelled by his unwillingness to forgive. Although Absalom's rebellion would only happen years later, it was the very first opportunity that Ahithophel had to get even - and he grabbed it with both hands. In short, Ahithophel succumbed to the boomerang of bitterness!

The crux of the matter is simple: Ahithophel had a root of bitterness that he simply would not deal with, and it ended up consuming him. A man who could have been remembered as one of the leading lights of his generation became known instead as one of the great traitors and failures of his day. I am not trying to suggest that David's sins were insignificant. Ahithophel had every right to be grieved; after all, he and his family had suffered a grave injustice at David's hand. Did Ahithophel have cause to feel injured, wronged? Yes. Was David's behaviour deplorable? Yes.

But bitterness is a different matter entirely. It clutters, clouds and contaminates the heart; it takes the pain and turns it into a cancer that eats away at the very soul until the person is consumed by it. Ahithophel didn't deal with the hurt – and it ended up destroying him!

Now the Bible expressly warns against the dangers of bitterness. It even speaks of bitterness as being something that both troubles and defiles a person:

> *See to it that no one misses the grace of God and that no bitter root grows up to cause trouble and defile many. (Hebrews 12:15)*

Indeed, God warns us to deal with bitterness by getting to the very core of it:

> *Get rid of all bitterness, rage and anger, brawling and slander, along with every form of malice. Be kind and compassionate to one another, forgiving each other, just as in Christ God forgave you. Be imitators of God, therefore, as dearly loved children and live a life of love, just as Christ loved us and gave himself up for us as a fragrant offering and sacrifice to God. (Ephesians 4:31-5:2)*

Why does God insist that we deal with the root of bitterness? Because He understands that it is a boomerang: It cannot be thrown by someone without coming back to cause that person harm! Somebody once put it like this:

> No matter how long you nurse a grudge, it won't get better. – Anon.

What Causes Bitterness?

Well, there can be many things that cause the hurt that causes the bitterness (and no doubt some of these things are very real and very legitimate wrongs), but ultimately, bitterness is an unyielding attitude, a deliberate decision to ignore the very counsel of God. If planted and nurtured, it will take root and sap the very life-blood out of its victim.

Jesus clearly shows us that bitterness is not inevitable. Rather, He makes it clear that bitterness is a choice made, not a consequence inherited. While on the cross, suffering the shame of our indignity, Jesus cried out, "Father, forgive them!" Jesus had every right to be bitter. Instead, He chose to show grace.

Living with a root of bitterness is akin to continually scratching open a wound so that it never gets a chance to heal properly. It is re-living the hurt again and again, replaying the injustice over and over, allowing the anger to fuel feelings of hatred and resentment; it keeps the bitter person bound, unable to let go, unable to move on.

We can't always stop bad things happening to us; we can't always prevent the actions and attitudes of others. As we journey through life, we are going to be injured. Some of those wounds will be the consequence of our own foolishness. At other times, however, they will be the result of the foolish and sometimes intentional actions of others. There are times when we will be victims.

However, wounds, if allowed to mend, become scars. While the scars remind us of what happened, they also serve to remind us that we have been healed. You can't forget the wrongs done, in other words; the scars remain. But they need not remain as wounds!

Allowing a root of bitterness to grow is like continually digging at the injury, opening it up again and again, causing it to fester. We never heal when bitterness takes root. It ends up consuming and destroying us.

Clearly, Ahithophel never let go of the hurt. When asked how he could provoke David, he told Absalom to lie with David's concubines in broad daylight – on the roof of the palace – the very place where David had stood as he gazed on Bathsheba bathing!

Ahithophel wanted to hurt David at his most vulnerable point; he wanted David to squirm in the guilt of his past sins.

Ahithophel may have taken his own life, but in reality, he had been killing himself a little bit every day!

When Bitterness Takes Hold

How do we know when bitterness has taken hold of us? In his book entitled, *'How to be free from Bitterness'*[11] Jim Wilson shares some wonderful insights. One of the signs of bitterness, he says, is that the person remembers the fine details of the event or events that led to their bitterness because they relive them over and over again in their minds, so to speak.

Incidentally, some doctors believe that replaying an event in your mind can have the same physiological impact on your body as though it had just happened to you. Bitterness causes us to remember the fine details because we literally re-live the moment over and over again. People become obsessed with what happened to them. It doesn't take a great deal to bring the conversation back to the moment.

Secondly, bitter people battle to forgive. They believe that they have a right to feel wronged and consequently do not see the danger in not forgiving those who have wronged them.

For all his wisdom, Ahithophel made a tragic mistake – he held onto the hurt, fed the bitterness... and suffered the consequences.

But as Christians, we do not have that right; we have been bought at a great price and we do not belong to ourselves. God implores us to let go of the bitterness, to bring it to Him and lay it at His feet, and to look to Him to give us the strength to move on. We cannot afford to become bitter about the injustices we have suffered. To do so is to be the victim twice over!

What is more, Jesus taught us that to be forgiven, we need to be willing to forgive:

> *For if you forgive men when they sin against you, your heavenly Father will also forgive you. But if you do not forgive men their sins, your Father will not forgive your sins. (Matthew 6:14-15)*

Finding the Strength to Move On

In Him we can find the strength to move on, to be free from the shackles of past hurts. It starts when we come to Him, burden in hand, and ask Him to help us to leave it there. We need to learn from His example, trusting that His Spirit will enable us to follow in unfettered obedience to Him. It is in learning to walk in His footsteps that we find the strength to be free.

Corrie Ten Boom, a lady who spent time in a Nazi concentration camp for hiding Jews in her home during the Holocaust lost not only her freedom and her dignity, but her beloved sister and father. Through God's providence Corrie was released due to a clerical error just one week before the other women her age were executed.

After the war, Corrie, a devout Christian and gifted orator, was invited to speak all over the world. She tirelessly travelled the length and breadth of the globe, thankful to the Lord for every opportunity to tell people about Christ. She always marvelled at God's infinite and intimate mercy toward sinners like us. She understood that mercy given to us needs to translate into mercy offered by us. She also knew, though painful, personal experience that it isn't always easy.

God taught her a wonderful lesson one day as she heard a church bell ringing in the distance. For the bell to stop sounding, she knew that the person ringing it needed to let go of the rope. This truth became tested in her life one day as she was ministering in Munich. In her book *The Hiding Place* she recalls the following story:

> It was at a church service in Munich that I saw him, the former S.S. man who had stood guard at the shower room door in the processing centre at Ravensbruck. He was the first of our actual jailers that I had seen since that time. And suddenly it was all there – the roomful of mocking men, the heaps of clothing, Betsie's pain-blanched face.
>
> He came up to me as the church was emptying, beaming and bowing. "How grateful I am for your message, Fraulein." he said. "To think that, as you say, He has washed my sins away!"
>
> His hand was thrust out to shake mine. And I, who had preached so often to the people in Bloemendaal the need to forgive, kept my hand at my side. Even as the angry, vengeful thoughts boiled through me, I saw the sin of them. Jesus Christ had died for this man; was I going to ask for more? Lord Jesus, I prayed, forgive me and help me to forgive him. I tried to smile, I struggled to raise my hand. I could not. I felt nothing, not the slightest spark of warmth or charity. And so again I breathed a silent prayer. Jesus, I cannot forgive him. Give me Your forgiveness.
>
> As I took his hand the most incredible thing happened. From my shoulder along my arm and through my hand a current seemed to pass from me to him, while into my heart sprang a love for this stranger that almost overwhelmed me.
>
> And so I discovered that it is not on our forgiveness any more than on our goodness that the world's healing hinges, but on His. When He tells us to love our enemies, He gives, along with the command, the love itself.[12]

Nobody understood more clearly how difficult it was and yet how vital it is to forgive others than Corrie ten Boom. Yet, in God's awesome enabling, she found the strength to do just that! If You are holding the rope and ringing the bell of bitterness, let go. If you are clutching the boomerang of bitterness, lay it down. God loves you too much to simply let you be the victim twice over. Let go and let God have His way. There *is* hope. There *is* healing!

9

Train up a Child

Text: *Prov 22:6*

Train a child in the way he should go,
and when he is old he will not turn from it.

As a parent, I have discovered that raising a child is a great blessing, but it is not easy - it requires hard work and sacrifice. Someone once put it like this:

> "Before I got married, I had six theories about bringing up children. Now I have six children and no theories!"

A further account tells of a young man who had graduated from university majoring in Child Behaviour. He subsequently took to the lecture circuit where he frequently delivered a lecture entitled, 'The Ten Commandments for Parents.' He later married, becoming the proud father of a new-born. When he began to lecture again, he decided a more appropriate title for his talk would be, 'Ten Hints for Parents.'

All went well until the arrival of his second child. His next lecture series was called 'Suggestions for Parents.' Finally, after the birth of his third child, he stopped lecturing altogether! [13]

Fortunately parenthood is not as bad as all that! While bringing up a child is a great responsibility which undoubtedly involves much hard work and sacrifice, it is still unquestionably one of the greatest privileges and blessings I have ever known. In his wisdom, God, who chose to introduce Himself to His Church as *Abba Father*, has given us some wonderful guidelines and timeless truths from which we can glean. It would be advantageous to take a moment to reflect on some of these.

Train up a Child in the Way He Should Go

It is my firm conviction that our chief responsibility as parents is to train up our children in the ways of the Lord. We can do them no greater service than this. But training up a child involves far more than simply reciting the letter of the Word without modelling the heart of it; Christianity, after all, is not so much a religion as a relationship. What better way to help our children cultivate a healthy relationship with God than to model one for them! As parents, our relationship with God must culminate in a deep desire to help our children to grow in their relationship with Him.

History teaches us that faith in God is not hereditary. Just because we might have a personal relationship with God is no guarantee that our children will automatically follow suit. What is more, simply sending them to Children's Church on a Sunday (as important as this is) or enrolling them in a school which claims to uphold Christian values (beneficial though this may be), is no substitute for our personal input. God gives *us* the command to train up *our* children in His ways. The lessons we learn from the offspring of Joshua's generation is a case in point:

> *After Joshua had dismissed the Israelites, they went to take possession of the land, each to his own inheritance. The people served the LORD throughout the lifetime of Joshua and of the elders who outlived him and who had seen all the great things the LORD had done for Israel.*

> *Joshua son of Nun, the servant of the LORD, died at the age of a hundred and ten. And they buried him in the land of his inheritance, at Timnath Heres in the hill country of Ephraim, north of Mount Gaash.*
>
> *After that whole generation had been gathered to their fathers, another generation grew up, who knew neither the LORD nor what he had done for Israel. (Judges 2:6-10)*

This passage arguably contains one of the most sobering Scriptures any parent will read. Joshua's generation had seen God do incredible miracles; they had witnessed how the waters of the Jordan parted so that the Israelites could cross into the Promised Land on dry ground and how the walls of Jericho had fallen supernaturally. Those who were born in the wilderness would have witnessed first-hand God's inestimable provision as He fed the nation of Israel day after day, clothing and sustaining the Israelites season after season and leading them year after year by the pillar of cloud and the pillar of fire.

Furthermore, taking possession of the Promised Land was well under way by the time these verses were penned. If ever one generation had reason to proclaim the wonders of God to another, it was *this* generation!

They were also known as a generation who served God:

> *The people served the LORD throughout the lifetime of Joshua and of the elders who outlived him and who had seen all the great things the LORD had done for Israel. (Judges 2:7)*

But a sobering verse follows:

> *After that whole generation had been gathered to their fathers, another generation grew up, who knew neither the LORD nor what he had done for Israel. (Judges 2:10)*

The younger generation did not know the Lord *nor* what He had done for Israel! It was bad enough that they had no personal relationship with God, but when one considers the fact that they did not even know what God had done for Israel, one is staggered! How is this possible? The only logical conclusion I can think of is that they were not *taught* these things - nobody took the time to tell them! Is it possible that everybody assumed that somebody else would do it?

I wonder how many Christian parents today actually take the time to talk to their children about God and what He has done in their lives. As important as it is to bring our children to Children's Church (or to send them to a Christian school where possible), let us not assume that, having done so, our work is complete. We cannot afford to make such assumptions when it comes to the spiritual wellbeing of our children - *nothing* can or should replace our personal input in their spiritual development.

Incidentally, this pattern of spiritual decline was not unique to Joshua's generation. A brief walk through history will reveal the same process repeating itself time and time again. It is not uncommon to see a generation of parents who were on fire for God raising a generation of children who were either religious at best or spiritually ignorant at worst. It is called the 2nd and/or 3rd Generation decline. Michael Stark puts it well when he says;

> "The first generation was holy; the second generation was religious; and the third generation was godless." [14]

Very often the first generation is marked by growth, the second by entrenchment while the third generation is characterised by decline. We cannot afford to be people who have experienced a personal, intimate relationship with God only to raise children who have a second-hand experience of Him at best, or who, at worst, have a third-hand experience in that they neither know Him *nor* what He has done!

Teaching on this very subject, Gary Inrig writes:

> "The Second Generation has a natural tendency to accept the status quo and to lose the vision of the first generation. Too often the second-generation experience is a second-hand experience. The parent's fervour for the Lord Jesus Christ becomes the children's formalism and the grandchildren's apathy."[15]

A similar pattern of decline may well be underway in Britain today. Recently our Sunday School teachers went on a training day where they heard a very troubling statistic. At the time of writing, it is estimated that only around 300,000 children attend Sunday School regularly in Britain.

Why is this so alarming? It is believed that 6 percent of our population attend church on any given Sunday (a significant decline from just a decade ago). This means that of the 3.6 million people who attend a Sunday service, less than 10 percent are children! If current trends continue, what will the Church in Britain look like just 20 years from now? We cannot *assume* that all is well - we must take God's instruction to heart!

Who Will Teach Them?

Why do we need to revisit our responsibility as parents to train up our children? For the simple reason that if they don't learn from us, they will learn from someone else! I know of a young boy who came home from his Christian School only to mention to his father what he had been taught during a Religious Education lesson that day. The teacher had told the children that believing in Christ was not essential. She told them that as long as they endeavoured to be *good* people, they could be assured of going to heaven. Bear in mind that this was a Religious Education lesson at a school that claims to uphold Christian truths! Her words contradicted the very teaching of Christ!

One could easily make the false assumption that because our children are going to a Christian school, they are being taught Christian truths, but making such assumptions could have dire consequences.

Let us not assume that what we learnt as children is what our children are being taught - we live in an ever-changing world after all. When all is said and done, if we don't teach our children, someone else will, and how *they* define good, sound doctrine may be poles apart from how *we* do!

Adopting the Spiritual 'Status-Quo'

Surprisingly, the children of Joshua's generation were not unspiritual - quite the contrary. What their parents failed to teach them they learnt from the Canaanites. Consequently they began to worship Baal.

Teenagers and young adults in Britain today do not claim to want nothing to do with God; many define themselves as 'spiritual, but not religious.' Few, however, are coming to Christ. Those who do attend church, see it as irrelevant. This does not imply that church *is* irrelevant, but merely serves to define their perception of it. Sadly, it is the very mark of an all-too-familiar pattern of spiritual decline. Michael Stark goes on to say:

> "The pioneers of the faith eventually age and they must surrender leadership to a younger generation... Gradually, the people seek acceptance in the community; and their brand of Christianity becomes "safe." The congregation grows satisfied with what they have and they no longer wish to jeopardise their standing. They... are no longer willing to risk themselves - what others may think of them - for fidelity to Christ.
>
> "However, concerned that their children are slipping away, the people look for more exciting programmes—programmes that do not demand sacrifice. Preaching that draws people back to the Word, demanding that listeners meet with the Risen Christ is

> counted as boring, and worship degenerates into a performance. How others might feel is important, but whether they actually know God is of no great moment. Parents doubtless mean well... but children so shielded are denied opportunity to discover the power of the Eternal God." [16]

It is my firm conviction that a nation who forgets the Lord will not be able to recognise what it has become. Let us help our children to see things for what they are because they are able to see God as He is!

Teach Them the Value of God's Word

It is not enough that we reveal God to our children; we need to ensure that we *accurately* reveal Him to them. Children need to learn the value of God's Word (not the opinions of men) because our opinions change from decade to decade and from generation to generation. Interestingly, when Paul wrote to Timothy about the value of the Scriptures, he mentioned the importance of being taught these from an early age:

> *But as for you, continue in what you have learned and have become convinced of, because you know those from whom you learned it, and how from infancy you have known the holy Scriptures, which are able to make you wise for salvation through faith in Christ Jesus. All Scripture is God-breathed and is useful for teaching, rebuking, correcting and training in righteousness, so that the man of God may be thoroughly equipped for every good work (2 Timothy 3:14-17)*

If we truly value God's Word, our enthusiasm will be contagious. Let us spend time in God's Word and encourage our children to do the same. Perhaps a time of Bible Study with our children, or a 'Question-and-Answer' session would help them to recognise the incredible benefits of time spent at the Lord's feet!

Don't be Afraid to Set Boundaries

We live in a day and age where people struggle to understand the importance of setting boundaries. But children need boundaries. Knowing the value of limits is vital to cultivating a sense of security. Nicky Gumbel shares a wonderful illustration about the benefits of boundaries. He tells of a time he went to watch his son playing football, only to discover that the referee had not arrived. Asked to substitute (and not knowing the rules very well), he reluctantly agreed. The game that ensured soon denigrated into chaos. It was only after the designated referee arrived, set out the boundary markings and began to referee the game properly that the boys began to enjoy it – the rules gave them the freedom to enjoy the game! [17]

The same is true when it comes to raising our children. The rules and boundaries we set with the help and guidance of the Scriptures enable them to enjoy life as God intended without the pitfalls and heartache that inevitably accompany disobedience and lawlessness. Children need the freedom that proper boundaries bring. As Homer Phillips put it:

> The time to start correcting a child is before they start correcting you.

Teach Them Value through Acceptance, Affirmation and Affection

Children need affection, acceptance and affirmation. Who better to cultivate these crucial components than parents? Our Heavenly Father uses this very pattern:

> *When all the people were being baptized, Jesus was baptized too. And as he was praying, heaven was opened and the Holy Spirit descended on him in bodily form like a dove. And a voice came from heaven: "You are my Son, whom I love; with you I am well pleased." (Luke 3:21-22)*

God the Father showed His *acceptance* of Christ with the exclamation, "You are my Son." He revealed His *affection* publicly when He continued, "...whom I love." He *affirmed* Christ when He proclaimed, "With you I am well pleased." The same pattern is followed during Christ's transformation – acceptance, affirmation and affection:

> *After six days Jesus took Peter, James and John with him and led them up a high mountain, where they were all alone. There he was transfigured before them...Then a cloud appeared and enveloped them, and a voice came from the cloud: "This is my Son, whom I love. Listen to him!" (Mark 9:2,7)*

As parents, we need to take time to help our children recognise just how much they are valued by showing them acceptance, affirming who they are and how much they mean to us, and making our affection known to them. Don't be scared to tell your children how much you love them. Verbalising your love won't kill you, but it will do wonders for your child's self-esteem!

Benjamin West, a famous British artist, first became aware of his own artistic skills one day when his mother left him to babysit his sister, Sally. In her absence, West discovered bottles of coloured ink. To amuse Sally, he set about painting her portrait. As young boys are wont to do, things soon became rather messy! But when his mother returned, she deliberately saw beyond the mess, picked up the piece of paper, and looked deeply into his eyes before exclaiming: "Why, it's Sally!" West would later say, "My mother's kiss made me an artist."

Someone expressed these very sentiments in the following poem:

If a child lives with criticism,
He learns to condemn.
If a child lives with hostility,
He learns to fight.

If a child lives with ridicule,
He learns to be shy.
If a child lives with tolerance,
He learns to be patient.
If a child lives with encouragement,
He learns confidence.
If a child lives with praise,
He learns to appreciate.
If a child lives with fairness,
He learns justice.
If a child lives with security,
He learns to have faith.
If a child lives with approval,
He learns to like himself.
If a child lives with acceptance and friendship,
He learns to find love.

- Anon

Learn to be a Good Listener

> *My dear brothers, take note of this: Everyone should be quick to listen, slow to speak and slow to become angry (James 1:19)*

As parents, our tendency is often to tell our children what they need to do. Sometimes, however, we need to remember that there are times when they simply need to be heard. We should endeavour to keep the lines of communication open by learning the importance of being a good listener, acknowledging what they are feeling, not simply what they are saying.

See time spent with your children for the invaluable investment it is. Charles Francis Adams, the 19th century political figure and diplomat, kept a diary. One day he noted:

> "Went fishing with my son today - a day wasted." His son, Brook Adams, also kept a diary which is still in existence. On that same

day, Brook Adams made this entry: "Went fishing with my father - the most wonderful day of my life!" The father thought he was wasting his time while fishing with his son, but his son saw it as an investment of time. The only way to tell the difference between wasting and investing is to know one's ultimate purpose in life and to judge accordingly. [18]

Pray *With* Them and *For* Them

Keep God in the relationship! Keep the love-triangle going! The closer we move together towards God in any relationship, the closer we will move towards each other.

Let us pray *with* our children. When we pray with our children, they learn to pray. Let us pray *for* our children. As we speak to the Lord about our children, we allow Him to speak to us about them. Through prayer, God is able to reveal to us things we wouldn't know otherwise.

Someone put it like this:

Dear God;
I don't know all of the challenges my (children) have,
But You know everything.
I hear their silence;
You hear their prayers.
I see their laughter;
You see their tears.
I see when they give;
You see what's been taken from them.
I see their beautiful appearance;
You see the scars in their soul.
I experience their faith;
You know their doubts. - *Anon.*

Speak to God about your children, and you will be amazed to discover that God will speak to you about them too! Never stop thanking God for your children. It is a reminder of just how valuable they are!

No Time like the Present

Perhaps you have a real sense of regret for lost time. You think about what you ought to have done (or ought to be doing) and feel a deep sense of having missed the mark.

While we may not be able to regain lost time, we are able to redeem the present time! Let us make a renewed commitment to God today to make the most of the rest of the time we have!

> Our lives are books and each day is a page. We cannot erase what has already been written, but we can always try to write a better ending with God's grace – Anon.

10

Transformed Transformers

Text: Ro 12:1,2

> *Therefore, I urge you, brothers, in view of God's mercy, to offer your bodies as living sacrifices, holy and pleasing to God—this is your spiritual act of worship. Do not conform any longer to the pattern of this world, but be transformed by the renewing of your mind. Then you will be able to test and approve what God's will is—his good, pleasing and perfect will.*

The ability of the disciples to see and understand truth was not inherent in them, but inherent in Him. As we have seen, the Scriptures made no sense to the disciples *until* Jesus opened their minds, even though they had already acknowledged Jesus as the Christ. God alone had the ability to open their minds. This should serve as a reminder that relationship with God is paramount to our ability to perceive and comprehend truth.

But God desires more of us than simply allowing Him to open our minds. He doesn't want us merely to be able to *see* truth as He sees it - He wants us to be completely *transformed* by what we see so that we, in turn, may be a catalyst in the transformation of others. How does God change us? He tells us:

> *"Be transformed by the renewing of your mind." (Romans 12:2)*

We are commanded, in effect, to *put on* the mind of Christ:

> *Rather, clothe yourselves with the Lord Jesus Christ, and do not think about how to gratify the desires of the sinful nature. (Romans 13:14)*

> *So I tell you this, and insist on it in the Lord, that you must no longer live as the Gentiles do, in the futility of their thinking. They are darkened in their understanding and separated from the life of God because of the ignorance that is in them due to the hardening of their hearts. Having lost all sensitivity, they have given themselves over to sensuality so as to indulge in every kind of impurity, with a continual lust for more.*

> *You, however, did not come to know Christ that way. Surely you heard of him and were taught in him in accordance with the truth that is in Jesus. You were taught, with regard to your former way of life, to put off your old self, which is being corrupted by its deceitful desires; to be made new in the attitude of your minds; and to put on the new self, created to be like God in true righteousness and holiness. (Ephesians 4:17-24)*

> *If you have any encouragement from being united with Christ, if any comfort from his love, if any fellowship with the Spirit, if any tenderness and compassion, then make my joy complete by being like-minded, having the same love, being one in spirit and purpose. Do nothing out of selfish ambition or vain conceit, but in humility consider others better than yourselves. Each of you should look not only to your own interests, but also to the interests of others.*

Your attitude should be the same as that of Christ Jesus: Who, being in very nature God, did not consider equality with God something to be grasped, but made himself nothing, taking the very nature of a servant, being made in human likeness. And being found in appearance as a man, he humbled himself and became obedient to death— even death on a cross! (Philippians 2:1-8)

Changed By What We See

We cannot see apart from Him, but God wants to do a far greater miracle than simply enabling us to see – he wants us to be completely transformed *by* what we see! If God is truly at work in our lives, a metamorphosis must take place. Jesus expected as much:

Then you will know the truth and the truth will make you free. (John 8:32)

The word 'know' in the original Greek is *epignosis* and literally means, 'to become thoroughly acquainted with, to know thoroughly through personal experience, even as we are known.'[19]

Changing How We Think, Not What We Think About

Jesus teaches us that we will know His truth intimately and personally to the point where it can be evidenced in our lives; we think *what* Christ thinks because we think *as* Christ thinks.

Putting on the mind of Christ involves more than simply putting on the thoughts of Christ. It is important to understand this. You see, transformation doesn't simply come about by renewing our thoughts; it is not enough to change *what* we think about. In essence, God is calling us to change *how* we think in the first place. The power of transformation does not lie simply in renewing our *thoughts,* but renewing our *minds.*

The Greek word for transform is *metamorphoō*, the root word from which we get the English word 'metamorphosis'. It literally means, 'to change into another form, to transform, to transfigure.' [20]

It is the same word as used to describe the transfiguration of Jesus. When we are transformed by the renewing of our minds, our way of thinking changes much in the same way as a caterpillar metamorphoses into a butterfly. We think differently because we *are* different! It is as simple as that!

The process of renewing the mind is much like the process of redecorating a house – the old is stripped away and the new is installed. Just as one wouldn't carpet over the old carpet when renovating a house, so we don't simply try to think new thoughts with the old mind. Rather, we are changed by God so that we *think* differently in the first place. God doesn't do 'make-overs' - He makes new! As we submit to the working of His Spirit, God opens our eyes to the truths of His Word and begins to remodel us according to His image. We are literally made new for His will and purpose.

As a Man Thinks in His Heart, So is He

'For as he thinks in his heart, so is he.' (Proverbs 23:7a - NKJV™)

Notice that the Bible doesn't say *what* a man thinks in his heart, so is he. Putting on the mind of Christ, then, involves thinking as Christ thinks, seeing as Christ sees, responding as Christ responds, speaking as Christ speaks, living as Christ lives and submitting as Christ submits. When our minds are made new, when we have put on the mind of Christ, this happens as a matter of course.

For the sake of clarity, let us take a moment to determine what we mean when we talk about the mind in this context.

The mind refers to our understanding, reasoning, thoughts, feelings, attitudes and will. So when God calls us to be transformed by the renewing of our minds, what He means is that we must not allow ourselves to conform (morph) into the patterns of the world, but to be transformed (metamorphosed) by renovating and refurbishing our understanding, intellect, thoughts, feelings, attitudes and will, starting again from scratch, allowing God to re-make us in the likeness of Christ. It is not simply a case of asking, 'What would Jesus do?' and trying to do likewise – rather it is a case of getting to the place where we respond as Christ would respond because we automatically think as He thinks, feel as He feels, see as He sees, do as He does!

We think like Christ, because we *are* Christ-like. We submit to His Lordship over our lives because we have been transformed by His example, seeing how He submitted to the will of the Father and doing likewise.

God's Will, *Will* Follow!

As Paul points out, the exciting reality is that this transformation enables us to know and discern God's will for our lives, His good, pleasing and perfect will. Unfortunately there are no shortcuts. We often want to put the cart before the horse – we want to know God's will first, and hope in the process that we will be transformed. But God says it works the other way round; we should concern ourselves with being transformed and in the process, God, in His grace, will make His will known to us. It will happen as surely as day follows night - we will know the will of God precisely *because* we have the mind of Christ!

God's desire for us is not that we try and discern what Jesus would do and then imitate Him. God is calling for far more than that; He wants us to get to the place where we don't have to wonder what Jesus would do in the hope of doing the same, but where we automatically think, see, perceive and respond as He would because we have *put on* the *mind* of Christ!

But what do we mean when we talk about the mind of Christ? Let us consider our Lord's example:

Jesus was Single-minded in His Purpose

Jesus could set His gaze like flint to Calvary because He was single-minded in His purpose. Presenting Himself as our sacrifice was the very reason for which He came. He was able to endure the cross precisely because it was the central mission of His life. Jesus knew that He had been called by the Father to be our substitute, our ransom; and as such, He had purposed to be about His Father's business.

His mission was never about Himself. He came to earth, not to be served, but to serve and to give His life as a ransom for many. When it came to the purpose of His life, Jesus remained resolute – God had purposed the cross for Him, and so He set His face like flint, determined to fulfil the life-mission which trumpeted the very heartbeat of God.

It is interesting to note that His ministry began with forty days of temptation in the wilderness, culminating in three named temptations. When one examines these in more detail, one is drawn to the fact that each temptation (on some level) was aimed at getting Christ to compromise the Father's will for His life.

Satan's first attempted to get Jesus to use His divine power to turn the stones into bread. This would have brought immediate gratification after forty days of hunger, but using His divinity for immediate gratification, for temporal gain, would have placed The Father's overarching purpose for His life in jeopardy. Jesus, however, would not compromise. Rather, His reply revealed a heart completely devoted and surrendered to the will of His Father.

Next, Satan tried to entice Him with authority and power. "Just worship me and all the kingdoms of this world will be yours. You don't have to endure the cross! There is an easier way!" But Jesus knew that His sole business was to be about His Father's business. Jesus replied: "It is written: 'Worship the Lord Your God and serve Him only." (Luke 4:8) Jesus never sought the kingdoms of this world because His kingdom was not *of* this world! The treasures of this life never enticed Him away from the purposes of God because His heart was fixed on God His Father. Where a man's treasure is, there his heart will be also! Jesus was single-minded in His purpose.

The third temptation involved trying to persuade Jesus to throw Himself from the temple, using His authority for His own preservation. Again, while this may have made His authority evident, it would have compromised the purposes for which He had come. Jesus displayed an uncompromising determination that His life would be about fulfilling His Father's will. He never sought temporal gratification, nor did He try to disguise worldliness in a righteous veneer, because He knew that it was not enough to simply be a sacrifice - His purpose was to be a *sinless* sacrifice!

Jesus was single-minded in His purpose because He was single-minded in His passion. He knew God's good, pleasing and perfect will and was able to fulfil it, not because of what He *thought*, but because of who He *was* (and is)!

God's desire is for us to present our lives to Him as a living sacrifice in the same way Jesus presented His life to the Father. Jesus calls us to follow Him as He followed His Father. As He took up His cross, so He invites us to take up ours. To put on the mind of Christ is to put on the determination to be as single-minded about fulfilling God's purpose for our lives as He was! It is not about us! It never has been!

Worldliness demands precisely the opposite. A mind set on the things of this world seeks the things of this world first. Then, if there is any time left over, perhaps the purposes of God could be addressed. But God says, "Seek first the Kingdom (authority, dominion, rule) of God and *then* all these things will be added unto you. Seek to be under the Lordship and leadership of God first!

Worldliness and godliness are diametrically opposed. Don't fall into the trap of clamouring after the things of this world, believing that this is God's will for your life. Get to the place where you acknowledge (as did Jesus) that your life is about the Father's will.

Jesus was Single-minded in His Pattern

No matter what Jesus did or said, he displayed the same commitment, character, compassion, conviction and consistency. There were no inner conflicts (to the pure, all things are pure!). He did not have to worry about being exposed as a hypocrite because there was nothing false about Him. He did not have to worry about having any hidden secrets revealed because there *were* no hidden secrets. Jesus walked and lived in perfect inner peace - His whole life displayed consistency precisely *because* His mind was fixed on God.

When tempted, Jesus didn't try to work out how He could 'bend the rules' and yet still get away with things. There was no inner conflict. He didn't have to worry about what to say because He spoke only what His Father told Him to say. Jesus always said the right things because He always thought the right things. He thought the right things because He heard the right things from His Father.

Jesus never panicked. We never read of Jesus becoming flustered. He was consistent. He was at peace - even in the storm. He slept while others stressed.

The lack of peace in the disciple's lives was not down to the presence of the storm, but the absence of peace. Jesus slept through the storm, not because He was peaceful, but because He was peace *full*! And so it is for the person whose mind is fixed on God!

Change Comes from the Inside-Out, Not the Outside-In

How do we know when we are being transformed? We begin to respond like the One in whose likeness we are being transformed! If I placed a can of cola on a shelf, it would respond as a can of cola should respond. If I put that same can of cola in the fire, it would respond as any can of cola should respond - it responds according to its composition. If we find ourselves responding like Christ in times of temptation or trouble it is because we are being metamorphosed!

Caterpillars transform into butterflies. As caterpillars, they are incapable of doing what they can do as butterflies. It is only after metamorphosis has occurred that they are able to fly, for example. They are able to fly, not because they *were* caterpillars, but because they *are* butterflies! It is natural for them to fly. They are able to do it because that is what they were made to do! That is transformation!

If we truly grasp what it means to put on the mind of Christ, to be refurbished in our attitudes, perceptions, thoughts, will and understanding, then there would be a lot less inner turmoil in our lives. And the natural by-product of a transformed mind is the ability to discern the will of God. We wouldn't have to question what God would want us to do or say because we would know it as surely as butterflies flutter! Do not be conformed to the pattern of this world, but be transformed by the renewing of your mind. *Then* you *will* know what His will is, His good, pleasing and perfect will!

Jesus Was Single-minded in His Priorities

Jesus had no distractions because He had *one* priority. People are able to say 'no' to something when a bigger 'yes' burns within them. Worldliness will always battle for our priorities, for the 'firsts' in our lives. 'Lord I will follow You, but let me *first* do this,' or, 'Let me *first* do that.' But God doesn't settle for left-overs! He shouldn't have to.

To put on the mind of Christ is to put on the single-mindedness of Christ; it is to be of the same heart, the same purpose, to embrace the same priorities. Worldliness is always about satisfying 'me'. Godliness is always about satisfying God.

A pond stagnates when there is no outflow because the pond was not designed for the sake of the *pond*. When we live for ourselves and not for God, we stagnate. The focus shifts to us rather than to God and what He wants to do *through* us. Life cannot thrive in stagnant waters indefinitely. Death and decay will follow. We were never designed to *be* our purpose – we have been designed for the plans and purposes of God. When God truly becomes our priority, the plans and purposes of God become evident.

Jesus was single-minded in His purpose, His pattern and His priorities. Such is the mind of Christ. Turning stones into bread never satisfies. Settling for the 'second-best' this world has to offer will never complete us. We were made by God and for God! Life on this revolving rock has never been about us (and never will be). The sooner we grasp this fact, the sooner we will realise the true blessings of God. Love, joy, peace, patience, gentleness, kindness, goodness, self-control – none of these fruits can be gained any other way than through a submitted, loving relationship with God through our submitted, loving Saviour.

Jesus taught us that where a man's treasure is, there his heart will be also. He set His face to the cross, but not for the sake of the cross - He set His face to the cross to secure the Father's greatest treasure. You!

11

Investigating the Heart of God

Text: 1 Sa 13:14 and Mt 11:29,30

"But now your kingdom will not endure; the LORD has sought out a man after his own heart and appointed him leader of his people, because you have not kept the Lord's command."

"Come to me, all you who are weary and burdened, and I will give you rest. Take my yoke upon you and learn from me, for I am gentle and humble in heart, and you will find rest for your souls. For my yoke is easy and my burden is light."

Our two Scripture readings are taken from very different times. The first Scripture recounts the events surrounding God's rejection of Saul as king over Israel because of his constant disobedience. Through the prophet Samuel, God rebuked Saul, informing him that He had sought another to be king in his place - a man after His own heart.

The second Scripture is an account from one of Christ's teachings. It holds a wonderful promise and is a verse which brings great comfort, particularly in times of trouble. And so we have two completely different verses from completely different times and circumstances. But there is a common thread running through both of these texts. Did you spot it?

Both verses make reference to the heart of God - the first text tells us that God chose David as king, not because of his many abilities, but because of his heart (simply put, David's heart resembled God's heart) - and in the second text, Jesus gives us a very small glimpse into the heart of God, revealing His gentle, humble nature.

Which leads me to the next question: What is the heart of God really like and how can we aspire to be people after His own heart?

More than a Pump

Whenever the Bible refers to the heart, it isn't talking about the physical pump in our bodies, Rather it uses the word in a figurative sense.

The Hebrew word for heart is 'leb' and means the centre or core of something or someone. The Greek word for heart is 'kardia' and refers to the chief organ of physical life. It was understood to represented the very core of a person. W.E. Vine defines 'kardia' as:

> "Representing a person's entire mental and moral activity, both rational and moral elements. It contains the 'hidden man' that part that truly reveals who we are without our being able to conceal it." [21]

So when the Bible talks about the heart, it is in no way a reference to the organ in our chests, but rather a description of that which is central, core and key to us. We respond, react, reason and reflect based on who we are deep down - we do this without really having to think about it.

Let us consider an example. We all have beliefs. We believe that some things are beneficial to us while other things aren't. But when that belief becomes a deep conviction, it impacts *what* we do and *how* we do it; it is, in effect, a deep conviction that comes from the very heart of us. We may believe that taking exercise is good for us. That is a belief. But when it is a deep conviction that comes from the heart, we will be compelled to exercise. Our heart beliefs make us do more than simply nod our heads – they cause us to roll up our sleeves and act.

The heart of someone therefore, is a measure of who they truly are, what they truly believe, and what drives them to action. It is not surprising, then, that the Bible makes a clear distinction between the heart and the mind:

> *Love the Lord your God with all your heart and with all your soul and with all your mind and with all your strength. (Mark 12:30)*

Jesus alluded to this distinction when He taught that a person speaks, not out of the abundance of the *mind*, but out of the abundance of the *heart*:

> *The good man brings good things out of the good stored up in his heart, and the evil man brings evil things out of the evil stored up in his heart. For out of the overflow of his heart his mouth speaks. (Luke 6:45)*

Indeed, He used this analogy to expose the hypocrisy of the Pharisees and Sadducees who often looked like they were playing the part, but whose hearts were clearly far from God. On the surface they appeared to be god-fearing, godly people, but deep down they were offensive to Him.

The Heart of the Matter

The Bible refers to the heart as being that deep part of us, the core part of us which reveals our true and often hidden thoughts, attitudes, desires, convictions, affections and motivations:

> *Knowing their thoughts, Jesus said, "Why do you entertain evil thoughts in your hearts? (Matthew 9:4)*
>
> *For the word of God is living and active. Sharper than any double-edged sword, it penetrates even to dividing soul and spirit, joints and marrow; it judges the thoughts and attitudes of the heart. (Hebrews 4:12)*
>
> *But I tell you that anyone who looks at a woman lustfully has already committed adultery with her in his heart. (Matthew 5:28)*
>
> *When he arrived and saw the evidence of the grace of God, he was glad and encouraged them all to remain true to the Lord with all their hearts. (Acts 11:23)*

How we perceive and interpret things is based on the condition of our hearts:

> *They are darkened in their understanding and separated from the life of God because of the ignorance that is in them due to the hardening of their hearts. (Ephesians 4:18)*
>
> *For this people's heart has become calloused; they hardly hear with their ears, and they have closed their eyes. Otherwise they might see with their eyes, hear with their ears, understand with their hearts and turn, and I would heal them.' (Matthew 13:15)*

God Searches the Heart

The Bible makes it clear that God knows and measures us by what is in our hearts - He is able to discern what really motivates us, drives us, what we truly think deep down. God literally knows us inside out!

> *Jesus, knowing their thoughts, took a little child and had him stand beside him. (Luke 9:47)*

As a man thinks in his heart, so is he. This is significant because we may be able to hide what we really think from the outside world (even possibly from those closest to us), but we cannot hide our thoughts from God. Have you ever wondered why two people can look at the same event and interpret it completely differently? We don't see things necessarily as *they* are, but as *we* are. To the pure, all things are pure. Why? Because it doesn't enter into their minds to think anything other than pure thoughts since their heart is pure.

That is why when God changes us, he gives us a new heart – He changes us from the inside out, giving us new convictions, motivations, attitudes and intentions.

The Heart of God

Let us turn our attention to the heart of God. Who is God deep down? What motivates Him? What drives Him to respond? What defines Him? If we are to love God with all our hearts, to seek to be people after His own heart, then what is His heart like?

When it comes to God's immutable attributes, we know He is perfect, upright, faithful, without injustice. We can be sure that when God judges, He judges justly. The fact is that God judges sin. We see it in the Old

Testament, and we see it in the New. When He judges, regardless of what our perception is, we can be sure that His judgement is neither unmerited nor premature.

But what motivates God? As much as God is a God of justice, He is equally a God of mercy. The very cross of Christ reveals both the justice and mercy of God at work; it is the only place where mercy and justice meet and are both fully satisfied!

God judges, yes, but it is clear to me that He does so when all other options have been exhausted. The prophet Jonah knew this all too well.

> *He prayed to the LORD, "O LORD, is this not what I said when I was still at home? That is why I was so quick to flee to Tarshish. I knew that you are a gracious and compassionate God, slow to anger and abounding in love, a God who relents from sending calamity. (Jonah 4:2)*

The psalmist echoed the same sentiments:

> *The LORD is gracious and compassionate, slow to anger and rich in love. (Psalm 145:8)*

The apostle Peter knew this to be true of the Lord:

> *The Lord is not slow in keeping his promise, as some understand slowness. He is patient with you, not wanting anyone to perish, but everyone to come to repentance. (2 Peter 3:9)*

It is clear to me that God allows us grace to repent before His judgement comes, because when His judgement comes, it is final. Before He brought judgement, He sent prophets to bring a warning, calling people everywhere to repent. The fact that we live some two thousand years beyond the cross is an act of God's mercy. God is a God of justice, yes. But His heart's desire is to show mercy!

A Heart Motivated by Mercy and Driven by Love

When it comes to His affections, God has one treasure – us!

> *For God so loved the world that he gave his one and only Son, that whoever believes in him shall not perish but have eternal life. (John 3:16)*

For God *so* loved the world... The word 'so' literally means, 'in this way.' For God (in this way) loved the world that He gave His Son Jesus Christ as our substitute, our propitiation. God's judgement was satisfied as our sin was placed upon Christ. His grace is offered freely to all who will believe in Him. That is the heart of God. And He did not wait until we were somehow acceptable to Him:

> *But God demonstrates his own love for us in this: While we were still sinners, Christ died for us. (Romans 5:8)*

A Heart Willing to be Emptied for Us

Have you ever considered what Jesus chose to do for us?

> *Your attitude should be the same as that of Christ Jesus: Who, being in very nature God, did not consider equality with God something to be grasped, but made himself nothing, taking the very nature of a servant, being made in human likeness. And being found in appearance as a man, he humbled himself and became obedient to death - even death on a cross! (Philippians 2:5-8)*

Jesus was born in Bethlehem. Why? It was in fulfilment of prophecy, yes, but God is the One who gave those prophesies in the first place. He could have chosen any city He wanted. But He chose Bethlehem. Why?

Today Bethlehem has around 27 000 inhabitants, but in Bible times, it was little more than an agricultural town, the smallest among the clans of Judah. The prophecy identifying Bethlehem as the birthplace of the Messiah alludes to *this very fact:*

> *"But you, Bethlehem Ephrathah, though you are small among the clans of Judah, out of you will come for me one who will be ruler over Israel, whose origins are from of old, from ancient times." (Micah 5:2)*

He grew up in Nazareth. Why? Nazareth was not the bustling city it is today. It was a small village of a few hundred people, located between two cities. It was in every sense of the word, one of those places you don't venture to, but drive through! Nathaniel the disciple revealed the attitude people had about Nazareth:

> *Philip found Nathanael and told him, "We have found the one Moses wrote about in the Law, and about whom the prophets also wrote—Jesus of Nazareth, the son of Joseph."*
>
> *"Nazareth! Can anything good come from there?" Nathanael asked. "Come and see," said Philip. (John 1:45-46)*

This is where God chose for His Son to grow up. Why? We can take it a step further; not only did He choose to be born in Bethlehem, to grow up in Nazareth, but God chose Mary to be His mother.

Now we know that Mary fetched water at the well, an undertaking which clearly showed that she was from humble circumstances – she did not have servants at her beck and call. Most theologians agree that Mary was probably a peasant girl, a poor maiden who was probably only a teenager at the time of Gabriel's visitation.

Yet the Bible says that Mary was chosen because she found favour with God (the word favour is literally the same word for grace; undeserved favour, unmerited love).

Jesus chose to be born in an insignificant town, to grow up in an even more insignificant town, to be born of a young maiden who in all likelihood was a peasant girl of humble circumstances. Why? Because of His heart!

God wanted to demonstrate to us that *nobody* is too small, *no* place is too insignificant, *no* person is beyond His gaze and *no* place is beyond His reach!

Every person ever born deserves judgement. We have all sinned and fallen short of the glory of God. But He died for every person ever born! God visited a 'nobody' in a place called 'nowhere' so that He could show favour to everybody everywhere! *That* is the heart of God!

Jesus Did Not Own Anything

Despite having occupied the very throne of heaven, Jesus chose to grow up owning nothing:

> *Jesus replied, "Foxes have holes and birds of the air have nests, but the Son of Man has no place to lay his head." (Matthew 8:20)*

God sent His Son from the highest place in heaven to the lowest place on earth, to find favour with a 'nobody' in a town in the middle of nowhere, to grow up owning nothing - so that He could give everything! That, friends, is the heart of God!

And the motivation for all of this? Immeasurable, undeniable, inexhaustible, unmistakable, indisputable, undeserved love!

God gave Himself up for love! His coming to our cross was God saying, "I cannot stay My hand of judgement forever. Justice must prevail. But I will give Myself to be judged! I will allow the full consequence of the stench and depth of man's depravity to be upon My head." And he did. *That* is the heart of God. *That* is love!

The Attitude of God

And consider for a moment just how Jesus received our judgement. He wasn't bitter. He didn't demand respect or expect payback – quite the contrary. After all, salvation is a gift given, not a tax enforced.

God gave Himself completely, yet still enables us to exercise the second greatest gift of all – the gift of choice. He gives us the right to accept His gift or to reject it. Even on the cross, the gift of choice was evident - one thief chose to receive the gift of grace and the other chose to reject it. Yet Jesus died for both of them.

He allowed the people He died for to spit in His face, to pull out His beard, to rip open His flesh, to mock Him publicly, to accuse Him unjustly, and then to denounce Him openly. He allowed His disciples to deny and desert Him.

During all of this, Jesus chose to remain silent:

> *He was oppressed and afflicted, yet he did not open his mouth; he was led like a lamb to the slaughter, and as a sheep before her shearers is silent, so he did not open his mouth. By oppression and judgment he was taken away. (Isaiah 53:7-8a)*

Jesus did not utter a single word in His defence. Why? Well, not only is Jesus described as the Son of God, but also as the Word of God. He was involved in creation, and He spoke the universe into being. The Word of

God spoke with immeasurable power. One word from Christ and a legion of angels would have come to His aid. So He chose to say nothing.

Jesus said nothing in His defence so that He could cry out, "It is finished!"

That, friend, is the heart of God! How grateful I am to serve a God who views us as His treasure! We love Him because He first loved us! He bought us back by His very blood, not so that we could be put on a mantelpiece like some inanimate object to be admired, but so that we can spend eternity getting to know Him, loving and being loved by Him!

May the fingerprints of our God be found on our hearts as we allow Him to fashion our hearts to be like His! May we be known as people after His heart!

12

The Unopened Gift

Text: Luke 2:1-20

In those days Caesar Augustus issued a decree that a census should be taken of the entire Roman world. (This was the first census that took place while Quirinius was governor of Syria.) And everyone went to his own town to register.

So Joseph also went up from the town of Nazareth in Galilee to Judea, to Bethlehem the town of David, because he belonged to the house and line of David. He went there to register with Mary, who was pledged to be married to him and was expecting a child. While they were there, the time came for the baby to be born, and she gave birth to her firstborn, a son. She wrapped him in cloths and placed him in a manger, because there was no room for them in the inn.

And there were shepherds living out in the fields nearby, keeping watch over their flocks at night. An angel of the Lord appeared to them, and the glory of the Lord shone around them, and they were terrified. But the angel said to them, "Do not be afraid. I bring you good news of great joy that will be for all the people. Today in the town of David a Saviour has been born to you; he is Christ the Lord. This will be a sign to you: You will find a baby wrapped in cloths and lying in a manger."

Suddenly a great company of the heavenly host appeared with the angel, praising God and saying, "Glory to God in the highest, and on earth peace to men on whom his favour rests."

When the angels had left them and gone into heaven, the shepherds said to one another, "Let's go to Bethlehem and see this thing that has happened, which the Lord has told us about."

So they hurried off and found Mary and Joseph, and the baby, who was lying in the manger. When they had seen him, they spread the word concerning what had been told them about this child, and all who heard it were amazed at what the shepherds said to them. But Mary treasured up all these things and pondered them in her heart. The shepherds returned, glorifying and praising God for all the things they had heard and seen, which were just as they had been told.

Christmas is a remarkable time of year, a time often remembered more these days for the hustled, bustled, frenzied scramble for last-minute gifts than the true reason we celebrate the season in the first place. But if you take a moment to look beyond the presents and the puddings, you will come to realise that it embodies the greatest moment in human history - the moment God became discernible, accessible and available.

Our Discernable God

Before Jesus' incarnation (and indeed, even at the time of His birth), most people had a very incomplete, inaccurate perception of God. Many perceived Him to be some 'divine dictator' who needed to be appeased. The worship of Molech, for example, demanded the sacrifice of a child, a grotesque and barbaric act that involved offering them alive in the flames.

People mistakenly believed that by giving a gift as valuable as this, their god would be appeased and all would be well in their world.

Still others misinterpreted God as someone to be feared rather than reverenced. The Israelites were too afraid to either write the name of God or to speak it publicly. Consequently, many embraced a stringent set of rules, regulations, traditions and laws which they believed needed to be fulfilled religiously, rigorously and repetitiously if they were to have any hope of appeasing this 'Lord of lists', this 'Majesty of mandates' and 'Divinity of demands'.

As far as having a relationship with God was concerned, people didn't expect very much. After all, what kind of relationship was there to be had when God was understood to be a tyrant who needed to be pacified or a taskmaster who needed to be obeyed rather than a heavenly Father to be loved.

Then came Jesus - and suddenly, God had a face! Here was someone people could look at, listen to, someone they could engage in conversation. And as they did, they began to see in Him the very heartbeat of God. Jesus put a face to God and what people saw overwhelmed them!

Here was One who was a far cry from some distant tyrant. Jesus, God incarnate, bowed to wash the feet of his disciples.

He was anything but aloof. Rather, He was a God who had chosen to step into our world. He knew what it was to grow tired, to be tempted, to weep. He knew what it was to feel pain, to suffer, to experience anguish. God stepped into a human world and saw life through human eyes.

Here was someone who spoke with unparalleled authority yet resembled the complete antithesis of a ruthless authoritarian. He befriended sinners and failures, showed love and compassion to outcasts, healed the sick and raised the dead - without demanding a purse for such extravagant acts of love. He embraced the marginalised and showed them how inestimably they were valued. He stepped into a world filled with hatred and taught by example how to love even those who had chosen to make themselves His enemies. Jesus *had* put a face to God- and that face was wonderful!

Our Accessible God

As we have already seen, God chose to be born in the most humble of circumstances to ensure that nobody was outside of His reach. Of all the places He could have spent His first night on earth, God chose a manger. Of all the people to whom He could have trumpeted His arrival, God chose to make this wonder known to shepherds - in a field - at night!

God had become accessible, and He did so as a humble, helpless baby swaddled in a manger! He became accessible, and chose to do so as humility personified. He came to a town of no consequence, to a lady of no social standing, had angels announce the birth to men of no status in a field with no significance. He chose to do this because He wanted, not simply to be accessible, but to be accessible to *all*!

Princes and paupers were equally welcome. Wise men and wanderers could all find a home. God wanted us to know beyond any shadow of doubt that no place is too small, no person too insignificant and no surrounding too lowly for Him. All are invited, and all stand on level ground at the foot of the cross. When Jesus came to earth, God became accessible!

Our Available God

By embracing life in our world, by putting on human skin, God made Himself available to us. He is undoubtedly the good Shepherd, the Great Shepherd and the Chief Shepherd, because He has lived among His sheep!

God made Himself available, yet He did far more than that. He came as our consummate gift to extend an unrestricted invitation. Jesus is the incarnate invitation to Himself!

> *"Come to Me all you who are weary and burdened, and I will give you rest. Take my yoke upon you and learn from me, for I am gentle and humble in heart, and you will find rest for your souls. For my yoke is easy and my burden is light." (Matthew 11:28-30)*

God has indeed become available, and He has extended an invitation to all. All may come. All may know Him. All may embrace this gracious gift, this mercy-filled miracle. All who choose to call on His name, who choose to put their faith in Him, will be saved - and we need saving!

The gift of God is not temporal; it is of eternal significance because it determines where we spend eternity. It is not a gift that holds *some* value, but *all* value. Jesus did not pay a *high* price, He paid the *ultimate* price. His gift is not *expensive*, it is *priceless.*

God chose to make His home with us so that we may make our home with Him!

Don't Leave Such a Precious Gift Unopened

Rodney Buchanan tells the story of a very wealthy man who had a passion for collecting art. His only son shared the same interest. Together they travelled around the world, adding many masterpieces to their fine collection; there were priceless works by Picasso, Van Gogh and Monet to name but a few.

Then war broke out and before long his son was off fighting for freedom. Sadly, after just a few weeks, the Father received a telegram informing him that his son had been killed while coming to the aid of a fellow soldier.

The following Christmas morning, the father heard a knock at the door. Opening it, he was greeted by a soldier carrying a large package. He introduced himself as the young man his son had rescued. He told the father that he was an artist and wanted to give him a painting he had done - a portrait of the old man's son.

Far from being a masterpiece, it reflected the skill of a young man still learning his trade. It paled into insignificance compared to the masterpieces hanging on the walls. Yet it captured the face of his beloved son in such detail that it soon became the father's prized possession.

The following spring, the father died. His passing was accompanied by the announcement that his whole art collection was to be sold at auction. The art world stirred with anticipation!

Auction day soon arrived and art collectors from near and far gathered in the hope of securing the rare handiwork of one of the great masters. However, many were surprised to find that the auction began with an unlisted painting - the portrait of the father's son.

When the auctioneer asked for an opening bid, the crowd remained silent. After a long, uncomfortable pause, he asked again, "Will anyone open the bidding?" But the restless crowd did not want to squander their money or their time on an unknown painting when so many great works were on offer.

Finally a friend of the old man spoke up: "I knew the boy, and so I would like to bid $100." With no other takers willing to better his offer, the auctioneer brought down the gavel, "Going once, going twice, sold!"

An audible sigh rang out. "Good!" someone exclaimed. "Now we can get on with the real bidding!" However, the auctioneer looked into the sea of expectant faces and announced that the auction was closed. "What do you mean?" came the puzzled reply. "We didn't come all this way to buy a picture of some old man's son! Where are the priceless works of art? I demand to know what is going on!"

The auctioneer replied, "It is very simple, sir. According to the instructions the father left in his will, whoever gets the portrait of the son gets the whole collection!"

I invite you not to leave the greatest gift of all unopened one moment longer! If you haven't already done so, put your faith in Christ and you will see in Him the loving gaze and eternal embrace of a discernible, accessible, available God!

After all, when you get the Son, you get everything!

13

Our Prayerful God

Text: Mt 6:5-15

"And when you pray, do not be like the hypocrites, for they love to pray standing in the synagogues and on the street corners to be seen by men. I tell you the truth, they have received their reward in full. But when you pray, go into your room, close the door and pray to your Father, who is unseen. Then your Father, who sees what is done in secret, will reward you. And when you pray, do not keep on babbling like pagans, for they think they will be heard because of their many words. Do not be like them, for your Father knows what you need before you ask him.

"This, then, is how you should pray:

"'Our Father in heaven, hallowed be your name, your kingdom come, your will be done on earth as it is in heaven. Give us today our daily bread. Forgive us our debts, as we also have forgiven our debtors. And lead us not into temptation, but deliver us from the evil one.' For if you forgive men when they sin against you, your heavenly Father will also forgive you. But if you do not forgive men their sins, your Father will not forgive your sins."

Prayer played a vital role in the life and ministry of Jesus: He was, and is, a praying Saviour. Yet the Lord's approach to prayer was revolutionary - it was unlike anything that people of the day had experienced - a world away from the prayers of the religious leaders of the time. The disciples saw in the life and teaching of Christ both an extraordinary example of and an unprecedented approach to prayer. Let us take a moment to investigate what Jesus taught about prayer and conclude by observing one of the most beautiful and heartfelt prayers ever prayed - the Lord's prayer in the Garden of Gethsemane.

Teach Us to Pray

The disciples came to Jesus one day and asked Him to teach them how to pray. He did. He started, however, by describing what He saw as the antithesis of prayer, revealing, by way of introduction, what *not* to do when praying.

Directing their attention to the prayers of the religious leaders of the day, Jesus warned His disciples about the pointlessness of hypocritical, attention-seeking, self-righteous prayers which were an affront to God; praying to be heard by others, seeking the acclamation and approval of men was the last thing that prayer was meant to be!

And so Jesus warned them not to pray like the hypocrites. The word hypocrite (hypokrinomai) means 'to impersonate, to play act, to feign, to pretend'.[22] It was a term which was used to describe actors who would wear a mask when playing a character in a play. God did not heed or desire the prayers of pretenders who sought to 'put on a show' as they pursued the approval of others.

Next, Jesus taught them not to use vain repetition and empty words. It was common for people of the day to pray to their idols by reciting memorised scripts and phrases, babbling incessantly in the hope that if they said the same thing long enough, loud enough and often enough, God would eventually get so tired of listening to them that He would have to accede to their requests - even if only to keep them quiet!

However, prayer, as Jesus revealed, was not an arm wrestle with God; instead, Jesus encouraged them to look at the way children interacted with their earthly fathers because they would see in this analogy a wonderful model for prayer. Our loving heavenly Father wants a relationship with us as reflected in a good relationship between a father and child. God wants prayer to be a sincere, loving conversation with Dad!

Talking about the prayers of children, I came across the following list of very amusing prayers children have prayed over the years:

Dear God,

Thank you for the baby brother, but what I asked for was a puppy.

I never asked for anything before. You can look it up.

- Joyce

Dear God,
Is it true my father won't get into Heaven if he uses his golf words in the house?

- Anita

Dear God,
I bet it's very hard for you to love all of everybody in the whole world. There are only four people in our family and I can never do it.

- Nancy

Dear God,
I like the story about Noah the best of all of them. You really made up some good ones. I like walking on water, too.

- Glenn

Dear God,
My Grandpa says you were around when he was a little boy. How far back do you go?

- Dennis

Dear God,
Did you mean for giraffes to look like that or was it an accident?

- Norma

Dear God,
In bible times, did they really talk that fancy?

- Jennifer

Dear God,
Please send Dennis Clark to a different summer camp this year.

- Peter

Dear God,
Maybe Cain and Abel would not kill each other so much if they each had their own rooms. It works out OK with me and my brother.

- Larry

Dear God,
If you watch in Church on Sunday I will show you my new shoes.

- Barbara

Dear God,
I do not think anybody could be a better God than you. Well, I just want you to know that. I am not just saying that because you are already God.

- Charley

Dear God,
It is great the way you always get the stars in the right place. Why can't you do that with the moon?

- Jeff

Dear God,
I am doing the best I can. Really!

- Frank

Dear God,
I didn't think orange went with purple until I saw the sunset you made on Tuesday night. That was really cool!

- Thomas

Of course, that is not to say that we have to pray precisely as children pray, because sometimes the prayers of a child (sincere and heartfelt as they are) can be slightly off the mark. But their unfettered love for their father and their unwavering trust in his ability is what our prayers should emulate. It is my firm conviction that prayer should be sincere, loving, intimate, respectful, heartfelt, personal – and real!

How Jesus Prayed

Jesus prayed addressing God as 'Father.' In fact, the term He used was far more intimate than that. Even in the Garden of Gethsemane (a heartfelt prayer in the very shadow of the cross), Jesus addressed God as 'Abba', an Aramaic term of endearment, which, loosely translated, means, 'Daddy'.

When Jesus taught about prayer, His opening phrase would have struck the disciples like a lightning bolt: He began teaching them to pray by encouraging them to begin with, 'Our Father'. Now bear in mind that this was completely unprecedented at the time. Until Jesus began to minister, God had only ever been referred to as Father in relation to His patriarchy over the nation of Israel.

In all, He is referred to as Father fourteen times in the Old Testament. It was a title marking the unique relationship with God and the descendants of Abraham, Isaac and Jacob.

The term 'Father' was just that – a title – a way of distinguishing the God of Israel from the gods of the day. But never had anyone considered approaching God in prayer as 'Father' until Jesus came along.

Yet in the Gospels, Jesus prayed to (and referred to) God as 'Father' sixty times. He wanted His disciples to understand that time in prayer was not some ritual to be followed but rather an intimate relationship to be cherished!

There is something very special about a child saying 'Daddy'! Having been given the great honour of being a father, I can say that few things bring as much joy to my heart as hearing my children say, "Daddy!" I awoke one morning to find my seven year old daughter standing at the bedroom door. When she saw me stir, she ran and jumped into my arms, exclaiming excitedly, "Daddy!" That was a good day!

And Jesus made it clear that God desires this kind of relationship with us! If we can grasp this wonderful truth, prayer will never be the same again! We will come to realise that it is not some chore to be painstakingly fulfilled (or some duty that needs to be transacted), but a privilege that needs to be embraced, a blessing that needs to be grasped: Prayer is the time we get to talk to Daddy!

Jesus' Unique Life of Prayer

Let us take a moment to consider how Jesus prayed:

Jesus was in prayer often. Sometimes He prayed long prayers that lasted through the night. At other times He prayed short prayers of thanksgiving.

Matthew 11:25,26 is a case in point:

> *At that time Jesus said, "I praise you, Father, Lord of heaven and earth, because you have hidden these things from the wise and learned, and revealed them to little children. Yes, Father, for this was your good pleasure. (Matthew 11:25-26)*

Sometimes Jesus prayed painful prayers. He knew what it was to pray in times of rejoicing and He knew what it was to pray in times of anguish. He prayed earnestly and sincerely:

> *Now my heart is troubled, and what shall I say? 'Father, save me from this hour'? No, it was for this very reason I came to this hour. Father, glorify your name!" (John 12:27-28)*

When Did Jesus Pray?

Early

> *Very early in the morning, while it was still dark, Jesus got up, left the house and went off to a solitary place, where he prayed. (Mark 1:35)*

Daily

We often read the phrase, 'As was His custom' in relation to the prayer life of Christ. Jesus prayed daily and taught His disciples to ask for their *daily* bread.

All Night Long

> *One of those days Jesus went out to a mountainside to pray, and spent the night praying to God. (Luke 6:12)*

The Gospels also record Jesus praying before making major decisions, before ministering, while ministering and after having ministered. Jesus prayed earnestly, sincerely and often.

Jesus Even Prayed With His Final Breath

His last words on the cross were words of prayer as He committed His spirit into the hands of His Father. Prayer played a major role in the life and ministry of Jesus. Should the same not be true of us?

A Model Prayer

Jesus gave His disciples a model for prayer. We could summarise it in the following outline:

Adoration – Our Father in heaven hallowed be Your name...

Prayer should start with praising God, thanking Him for His kindness towards us, and entering into His presence in loving worship.

Consecration – Your kingdom come, Your will be done...

Next, we set ourselves apart and submit our lives afresh to God. Our desire should be the same as that of John the Baptist – He must increase and we must decrease. The more we empty ourselves *of* ourselves, the more God can fill us with Himself!

Communion – Give us this day our daily bread...

Because God cares for us, He invites us daily to bring our cares and concerns to Him, to lay our burdens at His feet, and to receive from His hand a peace which passes all understanding.

Confession – Forgive us our trespasses....

Vessels of clay need to be washed from time to time. Let us keep short accounts with God when we miss the mark. Coming to God daily enables us to remember to walk daily in His presence.

Contemplation – As we forgive others...

God promises to use the same measure of forgiveness on us that we use on others. Let us be sure that no root of bitterness or lack of forgiveness is allowed to grow unchecked in our hearts and thus keep us from the grace God desires to show us.

Counsel – Lead us not into temptation, but deliver us from evil.

Jesus sent the Holy Spirit to us as our 'Parakletos', our Counsellor. Let us take a moment each day to ask God to counsel us, to guide us, to teach us and to lead us. If we give God the final say, He will not lead us into places of temptation just as a loving parent would not allow their children to be placed in compromising circumstances. Give God your car keys, cheque book and remote control. Let Him lead you – it will save you a world of sorrow!

Adoration – For Yours is the Kingdom, the power and the glory forever...

Prayer starts and ends with adoration and praise. We begin by placing God on the throne of our lives and conclude by recognising and acknowledging His Lordship over our lives.

Gethsemane Prayer

Jesus' prayer life and His teaching on prayer revolutionised the way the disciples understood and approached prayer. He helped them to recognise that prayer was the complete converse of a lifeless, repetitive ritual. Instead, it was heartfelt relationship expressed through respectful, heartfelt conversation with God. It enabled them to hear and to be heard. It gave them opportunity to speak to Daddy and to embrace His will.

Nowhere is this more clearly and aptly demonstrated than in the Garden of Gethsemane. In the shadow of the cross, just moments away from the greatest anguish He had ever known, Jesus the Son knelt before His Father and laid His heart bare.

The name *Gethsemane* is an Aramaic name literally meaning '*oil vat*', or '*oil press*'. It was a place where olives would be pressed and the oil extracted, which would be used, among other things, as fuel for lamps and lanterns. The heart of the Son was crushed in Gethsemane to light the way to the heart of the Father.

It is thus not surprising to find Jesus in anguish. With the weight of His impending crucifixion bearing down on Him, Jesus took Peter, James and John, three of His dearest disciples, to the garden to pray.

They saw Him as they had never seen Him before. Matthew's account reveals that Jesus was sorrowful. The English word, of course, does little to help grasp the depth of His despair. Three words are used in the Greek which give us a far clearer understanding of His emotional state, namely:

> λυπέω (pronounced loo-peh'-o) = to affect with sadness, cause grief, to throw into sorrow
>
> περίλυπος (perilypos) = intensive grief – to be overcome with sorrow to the point of causing one's death.
>
> And ἀδημονέω (adēmoneō) = to be troubled, to be in great distress or anguish, depressed [23]

The disciples saw Jesus as they had never seen Him before. Even in the face of the storm and the blood-baying crowd, Jesus had always been calm. Yet now He was thrown into anguish, overcome with sorrow to the very point of death, troubled with great distress.

Jesus reinforced what they had seen when He told them precisely how He was feeling:

> *Then He said to them, "My soul is overwhelmed with sorrow to the point of death. Stay here and keep watch with Me." (Mt 26:38)*

Luke expounds by telling us that Jesus literally sweat drops of blood. This was no figure of speech. Although this medical condition is relatively rare, according to Dr Frederick Zugibe, Chief Medical Examiner of Rockland County, New York, it is well-known and there have been many cases of it. The clinical term is hematohidrosis. Dr Zugibe states:

> "Around the sweat glands, there are multiple blood vessels in a net-like form." Under the pressure of great stress the vessels constrict. Then as the anxiety passes "the blood vessels dilate to the point of rupture. The blood goes into the sweat glands." As the sweat glands are producing a lot of sweat, it pushes the blood to the surface - coming out as droplets of blood mixed with sweat.[24]

If ever there was a time when Jesus needed His close friends, it was now! But even though He asked them to pray with Him, not one would honour His request.

Going a short way from them, Jesus began to pray. The cross was imminent, and in His foreknowledge and full knowledge, Jesus understood precisely what awaited Him.

Yet it was more than the physical anguish of the cross that tore at His soul. He knew that for the first time in all of eternity, He would be separated completely from the Father, cut off from His presence by our sin. The thought was an agony to Him. "My Father," Jesus cried; "My *Abba!*"

> *...My Father if it is possible, may this cup be taken from Me. Yet not as I will, but as You will. (Matthew 26:39b)*

Returning to His disciples, Jesus found them sleeping. Can you imagine how alone He must have felt at this moment?

Incidentally, how long did Jesus pray the first time? Matthew indicates that it was an hour.[25]

After calling His disciples to pray a second time, Jesus returned to pray once more. However, He didn't ask them to pray for Him on this occasion; rather, He warned them to pray for themselves:

> *"Watch and pray so that you will not fall into temptation. The spirit is willing but the body is weak." (Matthew 26:41)*

Jesus warned them that temptation was coming. They had missed the opportunity to pray for Him, but they could still pray for themselves. He encouraged them not to miss the opportunity.

Then, going off again, Jesus prayed a second time. What did He pray?

> *He went away a second time and prayed, "My Father, if it is not possible for this cup to be taken away unless I drink it, may Your will be done." (Matthew 26:42)*

Jesus prayed the same prayer, in effect. Then He returned once more to His disciples only to find them sleeping yet again. They had missed two opportunities to pray - once for Him and once for themselves.

However, this time Jesus didn't wake them. Instead, He returned to pray a third time. What did He pray?

> *So He left them and went away once more and prayed the third time saying the same thing. (Matthew 26:44)*

Jesus prayed the same prayer three times! While we do not know how long He prayed on the second and third occasion, we know that the first prayer lasted an hour. Given that He prayed the same prayer three times, it is possible that He prayed for nearly three hours!

After having prayed the third time, Jesus emerged. But something was different. Something had changed. It was not the circumstances, of course. The cross still beckoned. The cup had not been lifted. But Jesus was now able to set His face like flint to Calvary. A resolute determination had replaced a troubled spirit. Jesus had found the strength to submit to the will of His Father. He was ready to do what needed to be done. The Rock of Ages was ready to be the Lamb of God.

Gethsemane Prayer is 'Nevertheless' Prayer

The reality about prayer as illustrated by Jesus is that its purpose is not always to get us *out* of the situation we find ourselves facing. Sometimes it is about asking God to get us *through* it. Gethsemane prayer is 'nevertheless' prayer. It asks God to remove the cup, yet submits to and acknowledges His Sovereign right not to. It acknowledges that the cup of suffering might just be His will.

Suffering makes absolutely no sense to a mind consumed with temporal things. But seeing life from an eternal perspective helps us to understand that the troubles and sorrows we face here and now may be the very tools God uses both to change us and to challenge others.

Christian prayer is not pagan prayer. It is so sad that prayer has degenerated into making demands of God in so many Christian circles, as though God is some genie in a lamp on whom we call to do our bidding or to grant us our wish. Jesus never made demands of the Father; He accepted and embraced the eternal, sovereign will of the One who had commissioned Him to bear the sins of the world.

Gethsemane prayer was anguished prayer, but it was prayer which, through submitted obedience, turned weakness into strength. Gethsemane prayer was not selfish; it was selfless!

Pagan prayer is different. It says, "I'll do my part, God, and then You had better do Yours!" It does not consider the fact that 'nevertheless' may be central to the will of God for our lives. "Please remove this burden, Lord. *Nevertheless*, not my will, but Yours be done!"

Gethsemane prayer does not involve telling God what to do; rather it asks God for the strength to help us embrace His perfect will, even if it doesn't make sense to us at the time. It's not about me trying to change God's mind - it is about allowing God to change me if that is what is necessary. That is submissive prayer. That is Gethsemane prayer!

Jesus Prayed Preparedly

I am amazed that the Son of God, the One who calmed the storm with just three words, "Peace be still!", who called Lazarus from death to life with three words, "Lazarus, come forth!" who healed the cripple with just two words, "Be healed.", would find it necessary to pray the same prayer three times. Jesus prayed *until* He was ready to do what God wanted Him to do; He prayed *until* the purpose of His prayer had been accomplished. Jesus prayed *until* He had the strength to get through it, *until* He could set His face like flint to Calvary! It is a great lesson to us.

The cup was not removed; He would still have to drink it. He had asked the Father to take the cup of wrath from Him - and the Father had said no. But when Jesus emerged, the deep sorrow had lifted. The anguish had stilled.

Praise God for giving us such a vivid and important example both of the power and the purpose of prayer - If it is Your will, Father, change the circumstance. If not, change me!

Gethsemane prayer was 'preparation prayer'. Jesus had encouraged the disciples to prepare themselves for the trial they would have to endure. He asked them firstly to pray for Him and then encouraged them to pray for themselves so that they would not fall into temptation.

There are two questions worth considering here: Firstly, Jesus prayed three times, yet He took some of His disciples with Him and asked them to pray for Him. Would their prayers have made a difference to the number of times Jesus had to pray? One must assume so, or else Jesus would never have asked them to pray in the first place. While their prayers would not have removed the cup, they could very well have made the agony of the Gethsemane experience shorter.

Secondly, had they prayed for themselves when Jesus told them to, would they have fallen into temptation, denying and deserting Him? Again we must assume that their prayers would have made a difference or else Jesus would not have told them to pray in the first place.

Three friends should have prayed. They did not. Consequently, Peter denied Christ three times and all of His disciples ended up deserting Him. Is it possible that Peter denied Christ, not because it was prophesied, but because he lacked the strength to withstand the temptation when the trial came - precisely because He had failed to prepare in prayer when the opportunity had presented itself? If King Hezekiah's prayer changed the outcome of Elijah's prophecy, then one must assume that Peter's prayer would have made a difference!

The lesson is simple: The opportunity to pray is not something we can afford to pass up because opportunities to pray (as we learn from the disciples) are not limitless. Praying while we have time to pray might just make all the difference in the world! You see, we might only get one chance to pray for a friend in need. We might only get one opportunity to pray for ourselves before trials come upon us. Let us not neglect time in prayer, particularly when the Lord prompts us because we never know whether it will be the last opportunity to pray before the storm breaks.

Jesus Prayed Prior to Gethsemane

Incidentally, the prayers in Gethsemane were not the first prayers that Jesus had prayed that night. John indicates that He prayed before entering Gethsemane. In chapter 17 of His gospel account, John mentions that Jesus prayed for Himself, for His disciples... and for us!

Even in the shadow of the cross, in the midst of great personal anguish and suffering, Jesus remembered to pray for you!

May our prayer lives reveal a deep walk with our heavenly Father. May we be found in prayer often. May we be people who are passionate about prayer and who pray passionately! May we be selfless enough to pray 'nevertheless' prayers, praying until God changes us, even if our circumstances remain the same. May we pray purposeful, timely prayers. May we live to bring glory to our God and King!

14

The Abandoned Water Jar

Text: John 4:1-42

Just then his disciples returned and were surprised to find him talking with a woman. But no one asked, "What do you want?" or "Why are you talking with her?"

Then, leaving her water jar, the woman went back to the town and said to the people, "Come, see a man who told me everything I ever did. Could this be the Christ?" They came out of the town and made their way toward him.

It was midday and the Samaritan woman cut a lonely figure at Jacob's well. While it was customary for women to go together to the well to draw water at dawn or at dusk, she had learnt that it was easier to endure the scorching sun than the unforgiving glares of others. Poor choices and a chequered past had left her an outcast among outcasts. How sad that this place of refreshing could bring anything but refreshment to her. Instead, it served as a constant reminder that she simply didn't measure up.

An outcast among outcasts - she had endured the ignominy of being 'genetically impure' in the eyes of many Israelites. This came as no surprise, of course, given the seven hundred years of prejudice that existed between the Jews and the Samaritans at that time. Ever since the days of Ezra, when the temple was rebuilt, social interaction between the two groups was strictly taboo (a Jew would not even borrow the smallest morsel of bread from a Samaritan).

After Jeroboam divided the Kingdom, Samaria became the capital of the 10 Northern tribes of Israel. Through succeeding generations, the people became more and more idolatrous and corrupt until finally, in 722 BC, after many warnings from God, they were taken into exile. When they returned and re-occupied the region of Samaria, they became known as Samaritans.

The tribe of Judah (and part of the tribe of Benjamin) made up the Southern Kingdom of Israel. Although they enjoyed brief moments of spiritual fervour (unlike their northern compatriots), they inevitably trod the same path of spiritual decline until they too shared the same fate. They were taken into exile in 586 BC.

70 years later the tribe of Judah returned to Jerusalem and set about rebuilding the temple. The Samaritans (who considered themselves to be of Jewish descent and therefore eligible to participate in the rebuilding of the temple) wanted to help. However, the people of Judah frowned upon this, and subsequently refused them permission. After all, they didn't want 'unclean hands' touching the holy temple of God! And so the bitter trench of animosity that already existed between them became a crevasse!

Not to be outdone, the Samaritans decided to build a rival temple on Mt Gerizim in the north, claiming this to be the true place of worship.

To add fuel to the fire, a man named Manasseh, of the priestly lineage of Judah, married a Samaritan and was summarily expelled by Nehemiah in 432 BC. He went to Samaria where he was appointed high priest of the temple on Mt. Gerizim. The Samaritans began to offer sacrifices. In their nationalistic zeal they claimed that both their temple and their copy of the Law were greater than those at Jerusalem.

By the time Jesus began to minister Jewish animosity was so entrenched that a traveller invariably trekked around Samaria on his journey from Judea to Galilee even though this added a great deal of distance to the trip.

But such prejudice didn't bother the Samaritan woman anymore. It had become so engrained that she barely even noticed. No, it was the stain of being considered 'morally deficient' by her very own kinfolk that weighed heaviest upon her.

To add to her plight, not only was she a Samaritan, but she was also a woman. Jewish men of the day used to pray, "Blessed art Thou, O Lord... who hast not made me a woman!"

But this day would be different. A stranger, a man, a Jew would speak to her... and change her world forever!

Jesus Asked for a Drink

Jesus, God in the flesh, Holy God, awesome God, had deliberately chosen to travel through Samaria. Arriving at the well around midday, Jesus sent His disciples into the village to buy food.

Seeing the Samaritan woman, Jesus asked her for a drink. Imagine that! Here was a *Jewish man* asking her - a *Samaritan woman* - for water! How could this be?

Was this a chance meeting? Hardly. Our Great Master-Creator, the One enthroned above all time, had deliberately stepped into time for moments just like this! Jesus had intentionally journeyed through this unwelcome, inhospitable place in order to reach the centre of her heart. He knew precisely where He was, He knew precisely who she was, and *still* He asked for water!

Even more astounding was the conversation that followed. Realising that Jesus knew her most intimate secrets, yet was still willing to converse with her, she was stunned. Who was this man sitting before her? Surely He must be a great prophet! Perhaps he could settle an age-old dispute. Where was the right place to worship; Samaria or Jerusalem?

Jesus answered her, of course. But He had not come to settle theological disputes. He had come to open eyes, to loose chains, to heal hearts, to welcome weary, sin-stained travellers back to the Father-heart of God. As He spoke, her heart began to burn within her! She knew that Messiah would come - one day. When He did, He would be able to explain everything - just like this man...

As Jesus continued to speak, the scales began to fall from her eyes like the calluses that melted from her heart. He was right! It wasn't about *where* people worshipped, or *how* people worshipped, but *who* people worshipped. She could see it now! In fact, she could see more clearly than she had ever seen before! For the first time, this well, this place that had been a constant reminder of her shame, her guilt, her past, served as a wellspring of refreshing! Running home, she could feel the joy bubbling up inside her. She was healed! She was whole! She was home! *Joy Personified* met her at the well – and completed her!

She Left Her Water Jar Behind

> *Then, leaving her water jar, the woman went back to the town and said to the people, "Come, see a man who told me everything I ever did. Could this be the Christ?" They came out of the town and made their way toward him. (John 4:28-30)*

Now bear in mind that she had come to the well for the water she needed to survive, the life-liquid she needed to sustain her and her family - until the next visit.

But this day she completely forgot about temporal cares. What she found, or rather *Who* she found, made her unquenchable thirst, her constant striving, simply melt away. Her shame, her scourge, her past was finally behind her. For the first time in her life, she was free!

Have You Met Him at the Well?

How do we know when we have met with Jesus at the well? How do we know when our eyes have truly been opened? How do we know when our understanding of God is finally based on *truth* and not *perception?* It is when we forget our water jars at the well; when our steadfast strivings suddenly cease, when our pressing priorities suddenly change. It is when the guilt of our sin is finally washed away in the light of His love, when the weight of our past is silenced by the hope of our future.

It is when Christ suddenly becomes our desire not our duty; when we no longer need to ask which mountain to worship on, but instead want to bring everyone to the One at the Well where the living waters of God's love quench our thirsty souls!

Sadly so many Christians still suffer from the same misconception of God as did many living in Bible times. Like the Samaritan woman, many of us worship what we do not understand. We come to church and raise our hands - only to leave again, water jars in hand.

Many continue to clasp the burden of yesterday's guilt. We come, in many respects, water jar in hand, hoping for just enough to satisfy us until the next time, and then we go away again - water jars in hand.

Of course we have a *perception* of who Jesus is, we realise He is someone special, as did the Samaritan woman. We even understand *about* His grace, we know *about* His forgiveness.

We come to the Living Water - but instead of being immersed in Him, we come jar in hand hoping that just a little something will rub off, that we will feel just a little less guilty, a little less burdened, a little more satisfied - until the next time.

But Jesus didn't come to the well to fill water jars. He came to fill people to overflowing! He stepped into our world because He couldn't bear to leave us floundering as outcasts! He came as the Living Water, the Wellspring of Life. He came to set us free indeed!

Do You Know the One You Worship?

Don't sit in the presence of the King of Kings, singing about the limitlessness of His greatness and the wonder of His forgiveness only to go away again with less than all of Him. Our perfect, sinless, holy God stepped into time to visit *you* at the well, to wear *your* shame, to take up *your* cross, to receive *your* stripes, to taste *your* death, so that He could forgive *your* past, heal *your* present and secure *your* destiny!

Friend, your water jar cannot contain Him! When Jesus fills you, you will overflow! Water jars will never suffice! I want to remind you that the arms of the cross are always open - if it were not so, it would not be a cross!

Stop hiding from Him - He knows the most intimate details about you. And He is here, at the well – your well! Put the water jar down! The time for striving is over!

15

In the Shadow of Eternity

Text: Heb 12:1-3

Therefore, since we are surrounded by such a great cloud of witnesses, let us throw off everything that hinders and the sin that so easily entangles, and let us run with perseverance the race marked out for us. Let us fix our eyes on Jesus, the author and perfecter of our faith, who for the joy set before him endured the cross, scorning its shame, and sat down at the right hand of the throne of God. Consider him who endured such opposition from sinful men, so that you will not grow weary and lose heart.

The author of Hebrews writes an epistle to Christians who were largely Jewish believers struggling to live out their new-found faith in the midst of old religious traditions. While they had not yet resisted to the point of bloodshed (as had other Christian communities of the day), they understood what it was to be publicly maligned, ostracised and persecuted for their beliefs. Many had been forced to flee and some had even had their property confiscated – all because they had put their hope in Christ.

> *Remember those earlier days after you had received the light, when you stood your ground in a great contest in the face of suffering. Sometimes you were publicly exposed to insult and persecution; at other times you stood side by side with those who were so treated. You sympathized with those in prison and joyfully accepted the confiscation of your property, because you knew that you yourselves had better and lasting possessions. (Hebrews 10:32-34)*

And so the author writes to encourage them to stay the course, resisting the temptation to go back to 'life as it used to be', but to remain steadfast in the midst of life as it had become. He does so by using an analogy of an athletics race in which they were the chief participants, surrounded by a 'great cloud of witnesses'.

He begins the chapter with the phrase 'therefore', which connects what he was about to say with what he had just had written. In the previous chapter, he had listed the great heroes of faith. The author was trying to help them understand that it was their turn to take the baton and run the race marked out for them, just as the great heroes of the faith had done before, who now were spectators cheering them on.

He quotes many wonderful, inspiring examples in the process – Abraham, Moses, Joshua and David to name but a few. And now it was their turn; they were to run with the same courageous, committed and calculated determination, remembering that others had endured hardship and heartache, yet had stayed the course, finishing strong in the midst of great conflict and cost, straining with every fibre to win the prize.

He concludes the great faith chapter, however, by referring to those who had not received the fulfilment of the promise in their lifetimes, who had been sawn in two, left destitute, who had wandered around in sheepskins, living in caves because of their faith, yet who had remained steadfast despite their many troubles.

Secondly, the author encourages them to remember that their great Captain had also run the race. While reflecting on those who had gone before them would be helpful, what they needed most of all was to fix their eyes on the Author and Perfecter of their faith, Jesus Christ, who, for the joy set before Him, had fixed His eyes on Calvary, scorning its shame.

And therein lies a wonderful truth: Jesus endured the cross *for the joy set before Him*. The agony of the cross was made bearable because of the ecstasy to follow. Jesus knew that the heartache of the cross paled into insignificance compared to an eternity without us. He was able to endure the cross because He had our eternity in mind!

The Importance of Running with an Eternal Perspective

Knowing that eternity awaits helps us to run our race well! There is something so empowering, so liberating about living with the 'there and then' in mind.

Of course, that is not to suggest that we wait at the proverbial bus stop for the return of Christ. Living with an eternal perspective does not imply battening down the hatches and trying to hold the fort until our King returns! To the contrary, there is a race we have been called to run; it has already been marked out for us. We may not get to choose the route or the distance, but we do get to choose *whether* we run and *how* we run.

Running with an eternal perspective is saying, 'Lord, come what may, I am going to do everything in my power to ensure that I run well. I am going to throw off everything that has the potential to trip me up, and I am going to keep my eyes fixed on You, remembering that You were able to endure the cross because of the joy set before You! Running with an eternal perspective...

... Reminds Us Who Is in Control

Whether life suddenly takes an unexpected detour, or whether we are suddenly confronted with challenges we could never have anticipated, having an eternal perspective helps to remind us just who is in control. Regardless of the waves breaking around us or the storms billowing overhead, our eternal God is never caught off-guard. What He saw coming, He can see us through!

A good friend sent the following email to me a while back describing the accuracy of God. It reads as follows:

> God's accuracy may be observed in the hatching of eggs. For example; the eggs of the potato bug hatch in 7 days; those of the canary in 14 days; those of the barnyard hen in 21 days. The eggs of ducks and geese hatch in 28 days and those of the mallard in 35 days. The eggs of the parrot and the ostrich hatch in 42 days. Notice that they are all divisible by seven, the number of days in a week!
>
> God's wisdom is revealed in His arrangement of sections and segments, as well as in the number of grains. Each watermelon has an even number of strips on the rind. Each orange has an even number of segments. Each ear of corn has an even number of rows. Each stalk of wheat has an even number of grains. Every bunch of bananas has on its lowest row an even number of bananas, and each row decreases by one, so that one row has an even number and the next row an odd number.
>
> The waves of the sea roll in on shore twenty-six to the minute in all kinds of weather. All grains are found in even numbers on the stalks, and the Lord specified thirty-fold, sixty-fold, and a

> hundred-fold - all even numbers. God has caused the flowers to blossom at certain specified times during the day, so that Linnaeus, the great botanist, once said that if he had a conservatory containing the right kind of soil, moisture and temperature, he could tell the time of day or night by the flowers that were open and those that were closed.
>
> Thus the Lord in His wonderful grace can arrange the life that is entrusted to His care in such a way that it will carry out His purposes and plans, and will be fragrant with His presence. [26]

Living with an eternal perspective helps to remind us that God is in control. What He saw coming, He will see us through! Running with an eternal perspective...

... Helps Us to Accept the Right Invitations

In order to run well in the 'here and now', we need to keep a picture in mind of the 'there and then'. We only have a very short time on this earth and we need to make it count, because what we do on earth impacts what we will do in heaven.

The decisions we make this side of the grave have an eternal bearing on life beyond it. Jesus made it abundantly clear that eternity is intricately linked to present. In the parable of the talents, Jesus makes a vivid connection between earthly responsibility and eternal reward.

In Matthew 6:1 Jesus makes it clear that our eternal rewards are impacted not only by *what* we do here on earth, but also by *how* we do it:

> *"Be careful not to do your acts of righteousness before men, to be seen by them. If you do, you will have no reward from your Father in heaven." (Matthew 6:1)*

Revelation 22:12 emphasises the same truth:

> *"Behold, I am coming soon! My reward is with me, and I will give to everyone according to what he has done." (Revelation 22:12)*

Keeping an eternal perspective helps us to say 'yes' to the things that matter and 'no' to the things that don't. And when we consider how short life on earth is compared to eternity, it is worth thinking about. We will have responsibilities in heaven which are decided, in the main, by what we do on earth. Faithful service here leads to fruitful service there!

It is important to consider our eternity; after all, eternity is a long, long time! How long? Imagine that a woodpecker could fly to Mount Everest on the first day of each year and was allowed to take just one peck at the mountain. By the time it had managed to erode the whole mountain away, it would still not be the end of the first day of eternity! Keeping eternity in mind helps us to accept the right invitations. Let us run our race well! Running with an eternal perspective...

... Leads to a Defeated Grave, Not a Grave Defeat

If all you live for is life this side of the grave, then the grave is a grave experience indeed: We don't take our treasures and trophies with us, after all! If we only ever live for what we can get this side of the grave, then death is the ultimate hammer blow. But those who run this race to the glory and honour of Christ, keeping eternity in mind, know that death is far from the end! To borrow from a phrase Winston Churchill coined during World War II, the conclusion of life on earth as we know it is not the end; it is not even the beginning of the end; it is only the end of the beginning!

The Hebrew believers needed to be reminded that the loss they suffered presently was insignificant compared to the eternity that awaited them. They may not have chosen the race, but they did get to choose how they ran, and keeping eternity in mind would help them to run well!

And so the author writes to them and says, 'Keep your eyes on eternity just as Jesus did. Whatever hardship and heartache you are facing, as difficult as it is, run well!' Having an understanding of eternity is a great comfort and strength.

There is a very dear couple in our church who received the devastating news that the husband had developed terminal cancer. But rather than ask, "Why?" they both purposed in their hearts to make the most of every day God had granted them, knowing that God would give them victory, either this side of the grave or beyond it.

A few months later, the husband went to be with the Lord. Yet throughout that trial, they both proved to be an inspiration and an incredible source of comfort and strength to so many.

Having an eternal perspective helps us to keep things in perspective. We don't always get to choose the circumstances of life. But when trials come, when tribulations break, we can choose how we run!

Lawrence Lightbody was a man who ran his race well. Paralysed in a gymnastics accident while still at school, Lawrence was confined to a wheelchair for more than forty years. Many people prayed earnestly for his healing, including Lawrence. But healing did not come to him. However, Lawrence knew that life was far more than the sum of one miracle. And so he set about to make the most of every opportunity God brought his way. He had a Long Wave Radio and spent much of his time sharing the good news of the gospel over the airwaves. Consequently Lawrence touched and inspired many people through the years.

Standing in the church hall on the day of his funeral (standing because there was only standing room), it soon became apparent just how much of an impact Lawrence had made. Story after story was shared. Conversation after conversation revealed how Lawrence had touched so many people. A man who was unable to walk had walked into the hearts of hundreds! He lived with an eternal perspective, and consequently, made a triumph of such a great tragedy!

An eternal perspective leads to a defeated grave, not a grave defeat. Someone once put it like this:

> "Christians who have done the most in this present world were those who thought most about the next!" – Anon.

Describing eternity in The Chronicles of Narnia, C.S. Lewis wrote:

> "But for them it was only the beginning of the real story. All their life in this world... had only been the cover and the title page: now at last they were beginning Chapter One of the Great Story, which no one on earth has read, which goes on forever and in which every chapter is better than the one before." [27]

When a preacher was asked what had motivated him to do so much for God during his earthly life, he responded; "The smell of heaven has been on me all my life."

And so the author encourages the Hebrews to run with endurance the race marked out for them, fixing their eyes on Jesus, who, for the joy set before Him, was able to endure the cross.

Running with an eternal perspective...

... Helps Us to Consider Our Eternal Destiny

And there can be nothing more important than giving consideration to what Jesus taught about eternity. I know it is not popular these days to talk about, but Jesus taught more about hell than He did about heaven, and given the very mission of His life, this makes a lot of sense. The good news of the gospel is that Jesus makes eternity sure and secure! By God's grace, we don't need to suffer the consequences of an eternity without His forgiveness. We must give thought to our eternal destiny.

Thinking of the fullness and duration of this wonderful life, W. B. Hinson, a great preacher of a past generation, spoke of his own experience just before he died. He said:

> "I remember a year ago when a doctor told me, 'You have an illness from which you won't recover.' I walked out to where I live five miles from Portland, Oregon, and I looked across at that mountain that I love. I looked at the river in which I rejoice, and I looked at the stately trees that are always God's own poetry to my soul. Then in the evening I looked up into the great sky where God was lighting His lamps, and I said, ' I may not see you many more times, but Mountain, I shall be alive when you are gone; and River, I shall be alive when you cease running toward the sea; and Stars, I shall be alive when you have fallen from your sockets in the great down pulling of the material universe!" [28]

We may choose to live without Christ, but let us not choose to die without Him! Without an understanding of eternity, the cross of Christ makes absolutely no sense. But with an understanding of eternity, the cross of Christ is the only thing that makes *any* sense!

> A boy, just about to enter his teens, sat contentedly in the coach of a train travelling through the dry belt in the West. It was a miserably hot day but always he showed a smiling countenance. Others complained of the heat and the dust. Some found fault with the equipment of the railroad. Most of the passengers seemed out of sorts. It surely was not very comfortable, and travelling was most tiresome and uninteresting. The boy,

however, seemed to be enjoying the dried-out country, which to others had become most monotonous. An inquisitive motherly soul in the seat behind the boy was wondering what made the little fellow so cheerful. When she could curb her curiosity no longer, she leaned forward and asked, "Sonny, aren't you tired of this heat?"

"Yes, ma'am, I am a little tired. But I don't mind it much." The lady was about to ask why, when he finished his sentence, "Because, my Daddy is going to meet me when we get to Winnipeg!"

- Anon.

Our heavenly Father is waiting for us at the end of our journey. The road may be rough at times; no doubt we will all face hardship and heartache along the way, but thanks to His glorious grace and inimitable enabling, God will see us through - and welcome us home! Run well!

Discussion Questions

Chapter 1

1. How do people perceive the modern-day Church?
2. Are there ways that we can better serve our communities, and if so, what should we be doing?
3. What does the Bible view as living faith? (Read James 2:14-26).
4. What do you believe the author is trying to say in this passage of Scripture?
5. While we do not earn our salvation, since we are saved by grace through faith in Jesus Christ, is it true to say that faith finds expression in action, and if so, how are you actively living out your faith?
6. In what areas do you believe God is calling you to serve?
7. What are you doing to prepare yourself for service?

Chapter 2

1. Do we truly understand who Jesus is? Why or why not?
2. Is our conviction of who He is consistent with how He is described in Scripture, or is it possible that we allow our perceptions to cloud our judgement? Discuss.
3. What are some of the challenges we face in a modern-day, 'westernised' world that could impact adversely on our understanding of Christ? How do you believe this has impacted on your perception of who God is?
4. How do we allow God to re-shape our way of thinking?
5. What steps are you going to take to better understand the mind of Christ?

Chapter 3

1. After reading this chapter, has your perception of Thomas changed? If so, in what way?
2. Have you ever been labelled, either by others or by yourself? In what way?
3. Have you ever labelled others?
4. How does knowing that Jesus restored Thomas impact on your faith?
5. Are there others whom you know who might be living under a label?
6. In what way could you make a difference in their lives?

Chapter 4

1. After having read the chapter, what truth has stood out for you regarding the power of the tongue?
2. What do you believe God is telling you to do about the way you speak to others and what you choose to say?
3. How should we respond to a fellow believer who is spreading malicious gossip?
4. How should we keep ourselves accountable for the things we say?
5. Read James 3:1-12. What do you believe God is saying? What truth stands out for you? Discuss.

Chapter 5

1. What should we try to avoid when we become discouraged? Why?
2. What are things we should purpose to do with even more conviction when we are discouraged? Why?

3. How does knowing that God turned David's poor judgement around help you? Explain.
4. What thought stood out for you as you read the account of this brief period in David's life?
5. How has this helped you?

Chapter 6

1. How does understanding the geography of Galilee impact your understanding of this passage?
2. Does the knowledge that Jesus prepared a meal for His disciples in advance mean anything to you? Discuss.
3. In what way had Peter changed after the Lord's crucifixion and resurrection and what do we learn from this?
4. What have you learnt about the love of God from this passage of Scripture?
5. How does God's response to His disciples impact on our responsibility to fellow believers?

Chapter 7

1. What are we doing about making Jesus known in our circles of influence? Why is this important?
2. What thought do we need to give to present the gospel to people in our context?

3. What are some of the challenges the modern day Church faces in presenting Jesus accurately?
4. What are some of the pitfalls we should avoid as a group of believers that might give people the wrong impression about who Jesus is?
5. What could you be doing differently right now in how you make Christ known to others?

Chapter 8

1. Why is bitterness so destructive?
2. Why do you think God cautions us against allowing a root of bitterness to grow up?
3. Can you think of examples of people through history who have suffered serious harm as a consequence of bitterness? Discuss.
4. Can you think of instances in your life where you allowed bitterness to take root? What did you do about it?
5. Is there someone you still need to forgive? If so, why don't you ask God to help you right now?

Chapter 9

1. How does the lesson of Joshua's generation serve as a warning to us?
2. What assumptions should we avoid as Christian parents? Why?
3. How do you believe current patterns of decline can be reversed in churches in some western cultures?
4. Can you think of instances where acceptance, affirmation and affection from your parents helped to shape you?
5. What would you possibly want to do differently as a parent?

Chapter 10

1. How does putting on the mind of Christ affect our ability to discern the will of God for our lives? Read Romans 12:1-2.
2. Does the knowledge of God's overarching purpose for our lives impact on what we do for Him? In what way?
3. What deep conviction has God placed on your heart? Ask yourself – if I could only do one thing for God, what would it be?
4. What are you doing / going to do to fulfil it?
5. If the Church were really 'being' Church, what do you believe we should be doing?

Chapter 11

1. How does knowing about the heart of God impact you? Discuss.
2. What point in this chapter stood out most for you? Why?
3. God longs to show mercy. Does this have implications on the way we conduct our lives? If so, what?
4. Why do you believe God looks at the heart when choosing someone to serve Him?
5. Do you believe God calls the qualified or qualifies the called? Discuss.
6. How can we live as people after God's own heart?
7. What do you believe matters most to God? What are you doing about it?

Chapter 12

1. Jesus is God incarnate – God in the flesh. How does knowing this help you?
2. While Jesus is fully human, He is still fully God. How does knowing this impact you?

3. Is it possible, giving our human finiteness, that we sometimes put God 'in a box'? Discuss.
4. How do you understand Christ's invitation in Mt 11:28-30? Discuss.
5. What is most precious to you about the Christmas story?
6. What could you do differently for God this Christmas?

Chapter 13

1. What does knowing that God is a God of prayer do for you?
2. What do we learn from Christ's prayer life?
3. Discuss some of the ways God is challenging you regarding your prayer life?
4. What do you intend to do about it?
5. Do you find Jesus' model of prayer helpful? Discuss.
6. Have you ever experienced 'Gethsemane' prayer? Discuss.
7. Can you think of instances where God clearly prompted you to pray about something or someone? What happened?
8. What are the benefits of prayer?
9. Given that Jesus sometimes invited His disciples to pray with Him, do you make time to pray with others? Do you believe it is important? Discuss.

Chapter 14

1. Did you notice how the transformation of the Samaritan woman ended up being the catalyst for the transformation of her community. Why do you think this took place and why is it important?
2. Do you think it is possible to meet with Jesus yet not to truly understand who He is? What are the implications of this?
3. What are some of the prejudices and limitations that can keep us from experiencing the fullness of Christ? Discuss.

4. What are the dangers of prejudice and how can it affect our ability to be effective witnesses?
5. How should we deal with prejudice in our hearts?
6. What major lesson do you think the disciples learnt this day?

Chapter 15

1. How does having an eternal perspective benefit us?
2. Is there a danger of *only* having an eternal perspective? Discuss.
3. What does the Bible teach us about heaven and hell? How does this impact you?
4. Have you taken the time to consider your eternity? How does this make you feel?
5. Have you submitted your life to Christ? Why is this important?
6. If you are discussing these questions in a group, it may be a good time to reflect on what the Bible teaches about faith in Jesus Christ and to discuss this with your group leader.

Notes

CHAPTER 1

[1] The Message. Copyright ©1996 by Eugene Petersen, Mk 2:2
[2] Paul Alexander sharing statistics at The Christian Centre, NG, 2006
[3] Oswald Chambers: My Utmost for His Highest, Copyright ©1927 Oswald Chambers Publications Association Ltd.

CHAPTER 2

[4] www.gotquestions.org/Christian-worldview.html

CHAPTER 3

[5] Luanne Oleas in Salinas, Calif., *Reader's Digest.*

CHAPTER 5

[6] http://www.bible-history.com/hitchcock/Z/Ziklag/

CHAPTER 7

[7] www.biblestudytools.com
[8] Joel Edwards: An Agenda for Change, Zondervan ©2008
[9] Ibid.
[10] Ibid.

CHAPTER 8

[11] Jim Wilson: How to Be Free From Bitterness, Co-published by Canon Press and Community Christian Ministries, Copyright ©1995, Jim I. Wilson
[12] Corrie ten Boom, John and Elizabeth Sherrill: The Hiding Place, Bantam Books, Copyright ©1971

CHAPTER 9
[13] Source unknown
[14] Second Generation Syndrome: A Sermon by Michael Stark
[15] Gary Inrig: The Second Generation Syndrome – An Exigent Study of the Judges of Israel
[16] Second Generation Syndrome: A Sermon by Michael Stark
[17] Nicky Gumbel: Explore the Meaning of Life, The Alpha Course
[18] Silas Shotwell, in *Homemade,* September 1987

CHAPTER 10
[19] http://www.biblestudytools.com/Lexicons/Greek/
[20] Ibid.

CHAPTER 11
[21] W.E. Vine: An Expository Dictionary of New Testament Words, Thomas Nelson Publishers, Copyright ©1985

CHAPTER 13
[22] http://www.searchgodsword.org
[23] Ibid.
[24] http://www.christiananswers.net/q-eden/edn-t018.html
[25] Mt 26:40

CHAPTER 15
[26] Source unknown
[27] C.S. Lewis: The Last Battle, New York: Collier Books, ©1970, p184
[28] Walter B Knight: Knights Master Book of New Illustrations: WM B Eerdmans Publishing, ©1956, 1965, 1973, 1992 p555